Love, Sex, and Relationships

Series I

Love, Sex, and Relationships

Where Would We Be Without Them?

Ronald A. Hagen "Love Dr."

Writers Club Press
San Jose New York Lincoln Shanghai

Love, Sex, and Relationships
Where Would We Be Without Them?

All Rights Reserved © 2001 by Ronald A. Hagen

No part of this book may be reproduced or transmitted in any form or by any means, graphic, electronic, or mechanical, including photocopying, recording, taping, or by any information storage retrieval system, without the permission in writing from the publisher.

Writers Club Press
an imprint of iUniverse, Inc.

For information address:
iUniverse, Inc.
5220 S. 16th St., Suite 200
Lincoln, NE 68512
www.iuniverse.com

ISBN: 0-595-20996-3

Printed in the United States of America

FOREWORD

Building Relationships

In this day and age it is very easy to feel as if something is missing in one's life. We seem to be busier than ever, yet there can be an emptiness deep inside that we don't know how to define, much less fill. One way to fill that emptiness is by taking this opportunity to develop the talents, techniques and knowledge to develop a satisfying, exciting and romantic relationship.

This book outlines all the fundamentals to building a good and pleasurable relationship, and also explains the pitfalls to avoid. This book has what everyone needs to develop a sensuous and romantic relationship. All it requires is enthusiasm and the willingness to get started.

Learning about sex, Coping with sex, Unleashing your wildest desires and arousing new sexual pleasures. The secrets that drive men crazy, How to have multiple orgasms. How to "Super-Size" your sex life How to find out if you truly "know" your lover Unlocking the secrets to extraordinary foreplay Uncovering the pleasure zones Discovering what really turns women on. The techniques that will make your lover lust for you anytime, anywhere. The pros and cons of sexual dominance. The exotic worlds of aphrodisiacs and how they work. Techniques on manual stimulation and oral ecstasy. The positions of intercourse and why some work better than others.

The best part of all is that this book provides real strategies for real people. You don't have to be a professional athlete, a contortionist or a sex nut in order to experience the pleasures elaborated upon in our

book. All it takes is enthusiasm and a willingness to have red hot sex. Your love life is an emotional, sexual journey. Don't waste any more time on detours and dead ends. Love, Sex and Relationships is the map you need to find the passion you hunger for!

PREFACE

You are about to start a journey. This journey will develop an awareness of the components, methods and techniques that can increase the pleasure and gratification of a sexual relationship, thus creating a stronger bond and love affair. A long-term, healthy union is composed of many important elements such as commitment, communication, compromise, comfort and honesty. Without these components a relationship may start off with some sizzle, but there will be no bonding or staying power. **A successful love affair is a long-term commitment between two people that has numerous rewards.**

This book is a guide to help you distinguish between appropriate and inappropriate actions, behaviors and goals. Our aim is to help individuals develop satisfying, exciting romantic relationships. A happy relationship often proves to be a strong cornerstone in one's life.

The material in this book is meant as an informative educational guide. Nothing in this book should be considered as a substitution for sound medical advice or treatment.

The sexual techniques described in this book may not be appropriate for everyone. You are advised to discuss techniques with your partner before attempting.

Please have a medical exam and consult with a physician if you have any condition which precludes strenuous, sexually exciting activity. Some of the sexual techniques may take practice to do proficiently. Please proceed forward with caution and common sense.

Life is an emotional journey.

This trilogy can answer all of your questions regarding relationships, seduction and sex. It will prepare both you and your loved ones for the psychological and sexual adventures on life's journey.

INTRODUCTION

The seed of this trilogy was planted a little over a decade ago when I became involved with someone who harbored a great deal of anxiety towards forming relationships. I quickly came to realize that helping her overcome her fears required a great deal more than a general understanding of pop psychology.

Like many of my generation, I was searching for the secret of life. For years I had narrowly focused on obtaining wealth, power and fame. More than anything else I strived to be a success, both in the office and in the bedroom. However, once I accomplished these goals, I quickly found that rarely do these things in and of themselves bring any real contentment. Gradually I came to feel strongly that the real secret of life was to find and develop a romantic relationship that would bring about long term happiness and security.

I turned to books and research to find a solution for the anxiety that plagued my current relationship. After several months it became evident that the information available was woefully inadequate. This is when I began developing and researching the ideas that evolved into the work you now hold in your hands.

As with any factual piece, my work is in some cases extensions of ideas and research done by others. The material in this book has been formed from studies conducted by numerous organizations and from information provided by support groups, case studies, interviews and one-on-one tests.

The Great Lover Series is a self help program designed to aid individuals in obtaining successful, long-lasting, healthy, sexual relationships. To accomplish this goal, we have to use positive thinking to counter the rigid and deeply negative programming that so many have received as a result of our culture's exploitation of sex.

The second thing we have to do is break the sexual relationship into its major elements. *The Great Lover Series* defines the 24 major components of an outstanding relationship. We cover the actions and behaviors that harm couples, explain the sexual anatomy of men and women, define love, break down the art of seduction and analyze the role romance plays in a relationship. We discuss a woman's need for foreplay, the importance of good kissing and the secrets that turn men on. We show you how to become a better lover with techniques that create greater sexual pleasure and excitement. In addition we uncover the secrets behind having multiple orgasms and extraordinary oral sex and discuss how to master manual sexual stimulation. All the while we keep a steady focus on health and safe sex issues, and discuss the vital roles these concerns play in a relationship.

This may sound like a lot of information to cover, but keep in mind that the application of this knowledge can provide a lifetime of satisfaction and fulfillment. We will remove the **veil of secrecy** that has covered the topics of sexuality, physical pleasures and STDs.

You are bombarded on a daily basis by all forms of media exploitations of this topic. You've already been exposed to huge amounts of information. It is necessary to learn and understand the truth about the items in the trilogy in order to develop the behavior and thinking patterns necessary to obtain the goal you desire: a long term, safe, satisfying, enjoyable and rewarding sexual relationship.

CHAPTER I

THE JOURNEY BEGINS

Removing the Veil of Secrecy

Before we can begin to re-educate ourselves as to what comprises a meaningful sexual relationship, we must be able to let go of all of our misconceptions. We must learn to act on our own without the influence of preconceived ideas that have been established by the media. We need to put aside the erroneous beliefs and attitudes that have kept us from experiencing satisfying sexual relationships. In order to really experience fulfilling sex, we must be free of the labels and standards that society has placed on sexual relationships.

We need to be free to let our emotions flow when we interact with our partner. The passionate feelings and the fulfillment that we derive from a good relationship should not be inhibited by anxieties and fears.

The physical bond between two individuals can be like an emotional suit of armor. It can help protect us from the problems, frustrations and anxieties of our daily lives. In order to attain a level of freedom and remove the uneasiness from a relationship, we need to discuss what makes up the foundation of a good pairing.

Learn to Trust Yourself

The key to an enjoyable and passionate sexual relationship is to trust yourself and to not be afraid to experience and express your feelings.

However, instead of relying on our natural instincts, we learn to suppress our feelings because we have been exploited by the media. The media depicts what it believes sex *should* be like, not what sex actually *is*. They get away with it because our society, family, peers and religious organizations have created a veil of secrecy, hiding what a sexual relationship actually is. Thus we are unsure and afraid to trust our natural instincts.

Unfortunately, many of us never have an opportunity to learn what a good sexual relationship actually is. Many parents fail to teach their children anything at all about sex. Try as we might, it's not something that we can accurately pick up from films or magazines. Furthermore, discussion of sex is shunned in general by our schools and religions. Sexual energy is pure passion, the main life force directing our actions, and yet we are left unprepared and untrained to cope with this tremendous life force.

Many people suffer from their own distrust of their natural feelings and instincts and instead rely upon the media's image of what a sexual relationship should be. Almost everything in our society is associated or advertised with sex. Yet nowhere are we allowed to decipher our true feelings regarding sexual encounters and relationships.

Above all else, you must learn to trust your feelings. They will show you how to avoid mistakes and pitfalls while at the same time teaching you what you really need to know about yourself. This book has been designed to help you with this liberation of emotion.

The information presented here is not meant to be used for frivolous or casual sex. The goal of this book is to help you bring more security, excitement and joy to your love life.

CHAPTER II

ELEMENTS OF A GOOD SEXUAL RELATIONSHIP

A sexual relationship is as much an emotional encounter as a physical one. Thinking of another, anticipating meeting them, planning a romantic interlude or writing a loving note can be as much a part of the sexual experience as physical contact. A good relationship is comprised of innumerable gestures of loving, longing and kindness. Memories of such actions or special moments can be a person's most beloved treasures and can create bonds that last a lifetime.

In order to establish a healthy relationship, both parties must be emotionally mature and prepared and have a good attitude towards physical contact. Without these key elements no amount of physical stimulation or enticement will result in truly wonderful, satisfying sex. It is only in concert with one's mental and emotional state that one can truly experience the ultimate sexual relationship.

It's an unfortunate fact that people are unable to truly explain to another how to love, enjoy life or have meaningful sex. It's not something That can't be explained, it's something that has to be individually felt and experienced. Feelings are uniquely personal, and people must be able to receive as well as give emotionally.

Always remember that it isn't more important to please than to be pleased. One should not ignore their own needs and desires, or feel responsible to be a care giver. If you realize that it is as important for you to receive as it is to give, you will then realize that sex within a relationship can be very complicated. It is paramount that one shouldn't have false expectations or buy into the media lie that pure sex in itself is the ultimate. We must be honest with ourselves and then honest with our partners. Only in that manner will couples be able to express their desires, remove their fears and achieve the relationship that they desire.

In our many experiences with sexual relationships during our lifetime, we may find ourselves with a partner who is physically satisfying but emotionally empty. There may be great sex, but the lack of an emotional involvement leaves you wanting and feeling incomplete. This is because certain elements of a good sexual relationship are not present.

In a bad or abusive sexual relationship, one partner can be a giver, the other a taker. The giver can shower the other with love, care and sexual pleasure, but still receive little if anything in return. In such a situation, one partner is not emotionally able to receive and thus cannot give back to the other in a meaningful way.

From our experiences with support groups and interviews, we find that typically the woman is the giver. She can emotionally and physically give until she's drained, yet the man still will be unable to respond with the same level of care or emotion. There could be many reasons for this. It may be that the man is incapable of receiving, appreciating or responding because he isn't psychologically prepared. He may have a physical addiction like alcohol or drugs that warps his emotions and capabilities.

It's also possible that he may have unrealistic sexual or relationship goals. In reality such ambitions are forms of distorted thinking that cause unrealistic interpretations of events. This type of thinking typically distracts one from positive social conduct. It's also the reason that some set up mental barriers that prohibit them from responding to the emotions that are being given to them by their partner. This tremendous anxiety causes an emotional block and the man does not receive or respond to the woman. The result is that both feel their sexual relationship is wanting and unsatisfying. No matter how persistent one partner is, eventually they will become burned out. Thus you have break ups, separations, divorces or in some cases tense co-existences void of love or caring.

One element to developing a positive sexual relationship is to have good communication between partners. It's crucial that both are emotionally prepared to develop a pleasurable and satisfying sexual relationship. Without this mutual understanding and consent, the relationship will never be able to develop the solid foundation needed for a caring, long term commitment.

The Beginning of a Sexual Relationship

The sexual relationships of the new millennium are different from the traditional relationships of the past. Today people frequently leave their homes, families and churches to take advantage of career or educational opportunities throughout the world. As a result, we live in a nomadic society that makes it difficult for many to put down roots and leaves still more feeling isolated and lonely. Naturally, this makes it more difficult to develop a meaningful sexual relationship. The individual many times can become anxious, dissatisfied or apprehensive about sex. As a result, many become impetuous and rush into an encounter that is not fulfilling because the keys to a long term, satisfying sexual relationship are missing. Both individuals must understand the needs and boundaries of a sexual relationship and both must consent and contribute.

Mankind was created for love and sexuality. However, many of us in today's society seem to be stuck waiting for that "someone special." We languish in a state of limbo that neither furnishes us with comfort nor allows us to express our feelings.

Nearly everything in our society is geared towards couples and those who are sexually active. We are encouraged to share romantic moments, visit romantic places and experience true love and happiness. Society's single minded focus on couples and those who are sexually active is short sighted as well as misguided. As statistics show, the number of people who are alone and searching is increasing.

The data seems to indicate that we are becoming a society of individuals incapable of developing good, lasting sexual relationships. A new trend that has developed is for singles to attempt to emulate activities that have traditionally been practiced only by those who are sexually active. This is seen everywhere in the promotion of substitutes for sexual satisfaction. The outward sign that many people have extreme difficulty in developing full and rewarding romances is the proliferation of single individuals who attempt to have children without having a natural sexual relationship.

What does this mean for the individuals of the new millennium? Unfortunately it means that many are missing out on the significant contributions that are made to one's life from a rewarding sexual relationship. Many of the resources that life has given them lie untapped simply because they go undeveloped. Yet, many of the individuals of our new society are dying to be understood and loved by another. To avoid this pitfall, you must develop a formative program to prepare yourself mentally and physically for the development of a meaningful union.

Personal relationships are life's greatest challenge as well as life's greatest reward. In other challenges, we can usually identify the issues at stake, learn the skills necessary to work with the issues, develop a plan of action and then carry out our intentions with some effectiveness. However, with human relationships, especially sexual ones, we do not deal with logical or predictable entities, but with free individuals who can change their minds about anything at any time. Having a good personality and being able to have empathy with another does not necessarily mean the relationship will turn out well.

The first major step in developing a good sexual relationship is to understand that you can't dictate its course. You cannot control another's feelings. You may try. However, history shows that this never succeeds in the long run. Trying to control another's feelings many times will push that person away from you and will destroy whatever feelings you have for each other. In developing a relationship you must learn to adjust and understand. You must have empathy for the other person's feelings and needs. Find out what will make them fulfilled and happy, then incorporate these elements into your relationship.

Cardinal Rule

> **Life is ever-changing. Relationships must adapt to the change.**

What A Personal Relationship Is

The relationship is something very special. It is a unique bond between two individuals. None of us can deny the hunger and need for loving relationships. We want to be touched, listened to, taken seriously and comforted by another. We want a special person to share our feelings with, we want to develop a unique relationship and experience the euphoria of great sex.

When two people form this type of bond, their needs are properly met. We then experience a sense of satisfaction, happiness, contentment and completion. That is why when these bonds are broken we feel incomplete, angry and miserable.

Cardinal Rule

> You're going in the wrong direction in your life if everything is a priority except for your personal relationships.

The union between man and woman is recognized worldwide and endorsed by all religions known to mankind. When we accomplish this bonding, we are happy and many times the relationship gives our life a sense of true meaning. We can only experience this special relationship with another person whom we bond with. The key step in developing a good sexual relationship is to prepare ourselves mentally and emotionally to be open enough to trust another.

The steps that we are about to explain in this program are designed to help develop the proper concerns, awareness and thoughts needed to condition yourself for a sexual relationship. Further in the book we will explain the physical relationship with steps you can develop in order to enhance your sexuality. We will deal with all the senses: touch, smell, taste, and sight. However, unless one is emotionally prepared, you will never have a solid foundation for a sexual relationship.

A number of people have problems developing a pleasurable sexual relationship because they have anxiety disorders. Physical contact in general and rewarding sex in particular requires deep physical relaxation. If you're suffering from chronic nervousness or frustration, it's difficult to either receive or give pleasure, let alone properly develop a sexual relationship. Everyone from time to time will feel a little anxious about sexual contact. This is normal. However, there are those who suffer from anxiety disorders who become so keyed up and uneasy that they dread physical contact, even though in their hearts they long for a sexual relationship. This manifests itself in what is commonly called "performance anxiety."

Anxiety's devastating effects on sexual relationships are fully discussed in *Book Two* of the trilogy along with methods for recognizing, coping with, and understanding anxiety. In addition, it covers methods for overcoming anxiety and discusses the variety of prescription drugs and medical treatments that can be of assistance.

If you suffer from chronic anxiety, have unresolved negativity towards a prior relationship or consistently have apprehension and frustration regarding sexual contact, then you must read *Book Two* of the trilogy. A great deal of the information there will benefit your self esteem and ego and will enable you to enjoy all the pleasures and benefits of a good sexual relationship.

One of the major benefits of sex is that it stimulates the flow of adrenaline, the hormone secreted by the adrenal gland in times of stress. Adrenaline not only creates a rush of sensations such as tingling and pleasure, but many times it can leave a person feeling calm, relaxed and in a state of euphoria. These however, are only a few of the many advantages of having good sex.

The main thing to keep in mind as we discuss developing the proper attitude is to concentrate on the important stuff. Do not set unrealistically high standards or goals for yourself, and do not focus on the small flaws or errors you may have committed in the past. Rather, the important thing is one's overall progress towards their desired goals. You may want to review this concept several times until you feel comfortable and can put these elements into practice. The goal of this section is to increase your understanding of the necessary components needed to build a strong relationship while at the same time helping to increase your self confidence.

The first stage of a sexual relationship is physical. It's instinctive. It's biological. We will explore in this text methods and techniques designed to help you reach new heights of sexual excitement, arousal and pleasure. However, the second level of a sexual relationship is more difficult to recognize, comprehend and achieve. This level can be obtained by following the 24 steps described in this text. It is the level where people share a common emotion, a common bonding. It is not necessarily instinctive, and sometimes actions and feelings will speak louder than words. It is all of these components, chemical changes and attractions that make up the element of love.

CHAPTER III

THE STEPS: 24 COMPONENTS TO BUILDING A RELATIONSHIP

Cardinal Rule

> The most important decision in your lifetime is choosing the right mate and relationship because it will account for 90% of the happiness or misery that you will experience.

STEP 1—We vs. I

The first step in a sexual relationship is to start to think of things in terms of *We* instead of in terms of *I*. We all have distinctly individual thoughts, feelings, memories and sexual desires. Naturally, these memories and feelings are not identical to our partner's feelings. One must make the transition from thinking exclusively about themselves. It is vital to factor in the other person's emotions and goals as well. Thus you must start to make the transition from *I* to *We*. The relationship does not belong to you (*I*), it belongs to the both of you (*We*). There is a bonding between two individuals that becomes a part of each person's life. It is a positive feeling if the individuals can learn to share and accept the relationship on the *We*, rather than the *I*, basis.

STEP 2—Intimacy

The next element is intimacy. Intimacy means honesty, being able to be truthful to the other person in the *We* relationship. You may have to undergo an emotional evolution in order to develop a true emotional intimacy. You must be honest both physically and emotionally. This will bring about true unity in the relationship. You must be able to express your true feelings and desires. What things bring you enjoyment and pleasure? Where do you want to be touched? How do you want to be touched? What do you want done? Do you have frustrations or anxieties over certain things? Do you have uncertainties? Do you need help with certain things? Do you need time? Asking such questions requires a certain amount of honesty, first with yourself and then with your partner. You must be emotionally prepared to be trusting and to learn to accept the other person's emotional needs. When a person can develop this kind of intimacy, they will have a sense of belonging and receive comfort and satisfaction.

Unfortunately, many people in our society today develop negative bonds. They become close in a negatively emotional way. Similar to a family involved with an alcoholic or an abusive parent, the bond that exists is based on a sharing of toxic intimacy. Comprised of feelings of anger, hurt, shame, fear and frustration, negative intimacy can create powerful, long term connections. However, this is a destructive form of closeness. Usually people cannot survive in such relationships without sacrificing themselves and their true feelings.

Cardinal Rule

If a person cannot be 100% honest with you, then you are headed for an abusive relationship.

You must strive to have positive feelings in order to achieve intimacy and to experience a fulfilling, healthy relationship. This feeling allows people to become closer and closer until that bond enables the person to not only grow within themselves, but to also help the other person grow in the relationship as well.

Positive emotional intimacy generates an energy in our lives that passes on to others. Similarly, negative emotional intimacy creates a negative energy in our lives that touches the people around us. Thus you must be able to recognize the difference and correct or eliminate the negative intimacy of a relationship. You must end the negative intimate relationships in your life and replace them with positive ones.

STEP 3—Family

The third step or element is the family relationship. The person you're dating will many times identify with the type of emotional intimacy and energy that was generated while they were growing up. If that person had positive experiences, many times they will bring positive emotional intimacy to the relationship. If a person has had negative experiences, they will bring that experience and energy into the relationship. You must be able to recognize this because it will affect the development of your relationship. It is important that you spend time with your partner and be honest and ask them questions in order to develop a good understanding of their family unit and the interactions within that unit. If you or your partner have positive family ties, these ties will likely help you develop a strong union. However, if either partner harbors anger, anxiety or lingering resentment towards their family, then you must first learn to understand and cope with those feelings if you intend on forming any kind of lasting bond yourselves.

Cardinal Rule

> For a relationship or marriage to succeed, both partners must adapt to the issues of relatives, children, religion, finances and careers.

When you have developed the proper positive emotional attitudes towards family and sexual relationships, you will discover true self esteem and self confidence and will be able to bring to your relationship the concern and love that is necessary, while maintaining the freedom to express yourself. This will also be your guide to finding the right person with whom you can experience positive intimacy. In today's society, the great misfortune is that many times instead of looking for emotional intimacy, people look for pure sex, fame, power or wealth instead. These things often are mistakenly taken as being the cornerstones of a lasting sexual relationship. Unfortunately, when people use these goals to build their foundations on, they build on quick sand. Soon they find their foundations sunk beneath the weight of frustration, disappointment and anger.

Cardinal Rule

> You play a huge role in the transition of your partner into a new family. Don't criticize or undermine them. Reassure them and be positive when there are different culinary tastes, religious backgrounds or cultures. Attitude is the key to success.

STEP 4—Chastity

Having a sexual relationship is a voluntary choice. It will affect you emotionally and physically. If you chose not to be sexually active and want to protect yourself, then abstinence is the proper decision for you. Sexual thoughts, feelings and relationships are normal. Almost everyone has them. Sexual desires go along with physical and emotional development, so don't be embarrassed by them. Following abstinence does not mean that you do not believe in kissing, necking, petting, stroking or that you have to stay away from your partner. It means abstaining from sexual intercourse, usually until marriage. Some people feel that avoiding temptation is necessary to practice abstinence, and that it's not a good idea to get into a hot, passionate situation where you're going to be tempted to fulfill your urges. However, still understand that these urges and desires are normal and good. Abstinence has many rewards. It's a good basis for boosting self esteem. It allows you to be free of any worry or guilt. It guarantees that you'll be safe from all sexually transmitted diseases. It means that you have given yourself enough time to make sure you are ready for the responsibilities that go along with the act. Ultimately, abstinence allows partners to be more open and honest with each other.

Cardinal Rule

Safe sex is *not* 100% effective, only *chastity* is 100% protection for your most precious gift.

The status of one's virginity is a delicate topic that must be discussed in a meaningful way in order not to cause problems in the development of a sexual relationship. To wait to discuss one's sexual preferences and plans until one is in the midst of a steamy, passionate caressing session could cause some undesirable effects. One partner may feel rebutted by the other if they themselves are not a virgin. There may be a belief by one partner that the other is using their virginity as an excuse to not become involved in a deeper relationship.

Saying that one is a virgin at the inappropriate time will add to the confusion of a blossoming relationship. Before a developing love affair becomes too intense, discuss your feelings openly. Tell the other person what your true attitudes are towards sex and be direct in communicating to your partner what is agreeable to you. In this manner you can gain respect and admiration from your partner and the two of you can then work on the same level towards a meaningful and rewarding relationship. There is a wonderful and delightful world of sexual sensations and pleasures that can be enjoyed without having sexual intercourse. Until you are ready to make that commitment, you should be comfortable in the relationship that you are developing because you know what goals you want to obtain.

Cardinal Rule

> You do not create "LOVE" by having sex.

STEP 5—Ego

If you have or can develop a good ego you have enhanced your chances of having a rewarding, satisfying, happy, healthy, sexual relationship. When you're happy, pleasant and confident, you will generate a positive attitude that many times will overcome what can be major difficulties for others in a relationship, as well as instilling in your partner confidence and comfort.

Cardinal Rule

> A lover gives the one who feels loved a valid reason to feel self-satisfied, and instills self esteem.

You must recognize if your self esteem and ego are low or battered. If this is the case, you must work on developing a positive attitude. It takes patience and determination, but the rewards are well worth it. Having a positive attitude will also help you in matching up with someone who is in pace with your desires and needs. The results will be rewarding and positive for both of you. Know yourself and feel good about yourself before you unnecessarily worry about your relationship or your partner and their attitude. By recognizing this, you will be a much better person and a more capable partner in a relationship.

Cardinal Rule

> A bitter, depressed, unhappy single person usually will be a bitter, depressed, unhappy married person. Relationships do not usually transform people and their characteristics.

STEP 6—Patience

The key attitude needed for developing a good relationship is one of patience. Going too fast emotionally or physically can be damaging. One must be psychologically as well as physically prepared for sex. Remember, intercourse alone doesn't make a sexual relationship. You must be truly ready to make a number of different commitments. It is not enough for people to feel passion in a heavy caressing and kissing session and to express words of endearment. There must be true feelings behind the pretty words and steamy actions. People often say words of endearment during a hormonal moment. If you try to push a relationship, you may end up destroying it because you are moving too fast or too suddenly for your partner. You may develop feelings of guilt or of being used. It's very possible to end up emotionally scarred because the words of endearment that were said during a moment of passion proved to be false. Frustration, anxiety and hatred can set in very quickly in place of what you originally thought was love.

Both partners should take their time to really get to know the other partner's likes, desires, needs, feelings and sexual preferences. When it feels natural and right, you will know. Then, when it becomes time to make a real conscientious commitment, you will feel good about the decision.

STEP 7—Heart vs. Hormones

You must truly get to know your partner. Do your best to understand them, and take the time to find out what their wants, desires and traditions are. All too often the "honeymoon period" experienced in new relationships masks the true identity of one or both partners. Power struggles, major problems, disappointments and aggravations can all develop if you've been ruled by your hormones rather than your heart. Many times, in the heat of passion, when a man's testosterone is talking, things will be said that are not true or meaningful. Therefore, be ruled by your intellect as well as your heart. Do not let pure physical attraction be your main guide in selecting a partner, because many times this can lead to detours or dead ends.

STEP 8—Individuality

Being oneself is very important. This goes hand in hand with intimacy and honesty. It is good to be opinionated and to develop self interest. Independent thinking is a positive, attractive trait. To achieve a superior level of intimacy and honesty, you must know what you want and don't want, what you like and don't like. Don't hesitate to talk about the things that please and displease you. At the same time, always remember to express your love and have compassion. Always keep in mind that it's impossible to base a healthy relationship on deceit or manipulation.

Having common interests can greatly increase the longevity of a relationship. However, you must still be your own individual. You must be able to carry your own part and bring something to the relationship. Otherwise, it will become shallow, and over a period of time the love and care that were originally present will disappear. As we all know, we cannot respect someone if we do not feel that they are giving their own true feelings and opinions, but rather are merely mirroring the images or desires of others.

STEP 9—Communication

Cardinal Rule

> Therapists have learned that most couples that break up do not have the ability to speak effectively to one another, and thus cannot resolve problems. The reason for this can be because one or both partners are emotionally distraught and can no longer listen or empathize. Being too self-centered can also lead to a break down in communication.

In order to create a solid relationship, you must have a free flow of communication. The myth that sweethearts have an unspoken language or that they can "read" each other's thoughts or needs is simply not true. You may have empathy for the other person, but nothing can replace a simple and direct talk. One must clearly establish verbally what is going on in a relationship. We all know that it does no good to say to a loved one after the fact, "If I had only known."

Cardinal Rule

> There is always conflict in a relationship. Learn how to work it out gracefully. Sometimes *how* you say something is more important than what you say.

All the different steps that we have been discussing (self esteem, ego, honesty, intimacy) are tied in to being able to communicate your feelings and thoughts to your partner. Honest communication is essential. It's important that both partners in the relationship feel comfortable confessing their true feelings and desires to one another. So many people in our society, because of that veil of secrecy, aren't sure of their feelings or of their appropriateness and therefore never express them. In order to experience the pleasures and rewards of sexuality, you must be able to guide your partner. Try to feel comfortable enough to communicate to them what arouses you, what stimulates you, what pleases you and displeases you. Only by two way communication can both parties enjoy the benefits of a wonderful sexual relationship.

Honest communication is not easy for many. In fact, most find it's quite difficult. Furthermore, being a good listener is even harder. You must put in the effort and time to properly communicate. The following are some guidelines to help you develop good channels of communication.

- When you ask a question, give your partner a chance to answer.
- Don't ask questions that lack realistic or practical answers.
- Take turns.
- Don't get into heated arguments regarding children or jobs.
- Always listen with an open mind and be realistic about your decisions.
- If you can't agree, try to find middle ground. Learn to compromise. Compromising is the secret to eliminating frustration while building a good relationship.

When the opportunity presents itself, relax. Learn to laugh at small problems or faults. In other words, "do not sweat the small stuff." Do not criticize or complain. There is no advantage to be gained through criticism, and it ultimately will undermine honest communication. Give your mate the opportunity to think things over and then make a decision and respond. Do not pressure them into making decisions. Be optimistic and lighthearted. Sometimes a problem is only serious in a person's mind. Always cultivate understanding and forgiveness. If you truly put effort and time into your love affair, then good communication will naturally follow.

Remember, many times there is no right or wrong, no "yes" or "no" answer. Sometimes the solution to a problem isn't obvious or simple and many times there is no quick fix. The virtues of patience and cooperation can help couples work out compromises or solutions that allow everyone to be happy.

Cardinal Rule

Never verbally attack your mate. In the future they will be unwilling to open up to you about themselves. Eventually, they may stop listening to what you have to say all together.

STEP 10—Candor

In order for your relationship to have staying power, you must understand that there will always be a difference between you and your partner, and that you will never have all the same likes and dislikes. However, variety can be a good ingredient in your relationship if you can be realistic and accept the other person's beliefs, desires and faults.

If you are unrealistic about what a relationship should be and cannot accept the other person for their true self, then you will never be able to overcome the small problems that life places in front of each of us. How he or she looks in the morning is part of life. Occasionally each partner may do something silly, frivolous or stupid. You must have enough candor to express your thoughts and feelings about these items and learn to accept and overcome them. If you continually force major confrontations over minor issues, you will soon place a tremendous hardship on the relationship and each partner will become very critical of the other. In a good relationship there must be some give and take. It is that element, that empathy, that helps make the bonding so much stronger. If you make too much of the small stuff, you will never be able to overcome the major obstacles that life will throw in front of you, and you will commit yourself to disappointment and failure in your relationship.

Cardinal Rule

No one wants to be alone. Respect the other person's beliefs and concerns.

STEP 11—Ground Rules

If you want your relationship to thrive, then you must discuss the ground rules that will develop its framework. A healthy relationship will foster good communication and mutual respect. The ground rules that you discuss with your partner are essential to forming a long term commitment. The old proverb that love will change things does not really hold true in most cases. If your partner is doing something that is offensive or hurts you early in your relationship, you must discuss it and set up a ground rule. Otherwise, your patience will wear thinner and thinner and your aggravation will grow greater and greater as time goes on. Some people, especially younger people, believe that if they wait things will get better or that the person will change. More times than not, this is not the case. Conflicts that seem minor in the beginning can become major points of resentment later.

It's good to be understanding and forgiving. However, couples will develop problems in their relationship if they don't have certain ground rules and respect for each other's feelings. Here are some basic tips for helping you shape your own set of ground rules:

- Never exert pressure on your partner to do something that they are not mentally, emotionally or physically ready to do.
- Never argue or belittle your partner in front of friends, family or in public.
- Learn to discuss your problems and true feelings, even if it's easier to lie.
- Have empathy for your partner's feelings and needs. Don't belittle their desires or dismiss their questions and requests.
- Try to never fight or argue while having sex.
- Establish some quiet time when you can sit with your partner and discuss any questions or problems.
- Keep a regular channel of communication open.

Establishing some ground rules in a love affair is very important. It will enable you to maintain respect for yourself and your partner along with helping you both avoid the mistakes that weaken or destroy relationships.

Cardinal Rule

> To reach your goal, you need to put in both effort and time.

STEP 12—Bonding

Love is usually thought of as a carefree, wonderful time. However, lovers face many difficult times and obstacles. The real test of devotion is how well people bond together in times of adversity or stress. If the elements of a good relationship are in place, people will come together and support each other during trying times. The bonding process will help you overcome the grief, difficulty or struggle that you are facing.

If these elements aren't in place, the typical pattern is for people to distance themselves from each other. During a period of difficulty, whether emotional, physical or financial, people will backslide or even abandon their partners. The issue of bonding has even come under the scrutiny of the medical community in recent years. Current studies show that people who are in strong, secure, loving relationships have an easier time surmounting all manner of difficulties and tragedies. Data from the insurance industry supports reports that people living together in a relationship have a tendency to live longer than those who are isolated and alone. There are now numerous articles in medical digests stating that people have a tendency to heal and recuperate better and faster when they are at home in the care of loved ones rather than in hospitals or institutions.

Cardinal Rule

> Sex is not the only bond between a couple. It is essential to make the effort to focus on each other's needs, wants, desires, problems, dreams and plans for the future. By being honest and intimate and sharing your feelings, you create and retain many bonds.

The relationship will develop into the whole of its elements. If you and your lover are practicing the right steps and are right for one another, then you will be able to develop a bond that will remain through thick and thin. Such a union can be a source of great strength for each individual. That same bond can also encourage people to perform way beyond their normal capacity in a situation.

STEP 13—Don't Criticize

One of the problems that comes about early in a relationship is when one partner tries to change the other. If you truly care for the person, you must follow the other steps involved in nurturing a relationship, such as maintaining open lines of communication and setting ground rules. Once this is done, you must learn to deal with and understand the other person's viewpoints and characteristics. If you don't accept these traits, then never attempt to criticize or change the person. Criticizing causes a lot of relationships to break up.

Cardinal Rule

> Do not destroy your relationship by putting too much pressure on it.

If you and your partner aren't compatible, it's important to try to recognize it early in the relationship and let it end. You will be on track for a lot of emotional difficulty if you persist in trying to change a person's character by criticism and you will only end up causing a lot of anger, frustration and hatred. If the relationship is only skin deep, having sizzle but little substance, you cannot prolong it by trying to mold someone into the type of person you would like. If you wish to have a long term love affair with someone, then you must be able to understand their character and their passions. Knowing that their values are accepted and understood will bolster your partner's self worth. This is a major requirement for falling in love. Recognize this element early in your relationship. A common reason that couples break up is because one partner will attempt to change the other's actions or attitudes.

STEP 14—Saying You're Sorry

It is better to say you're sorry than to be sorry you didn't say it. All relationships will have times of conflict. It is how you handle the conflict that's important, more important many times than what you're actually arguing about. Over time, people have a tendency to forget what they were fighting about, but they remember the harsh words or the results of an argument. It's important not to distort the facts, make generalizations, pull in prior events or relationships, or belittle the other person and their viewpoint or comments. You must learn to argue fairly and to express your problems and concerns without becoming a dirty fighter. Express your feelings when you're angry, but do so constructively and allow the other person an opportunity to understand and to make amends. Always allow the opportunity for your partner to apologize. Once they have taken that step, you must be in a position to forgive and move forward.

A major obstacle to many relationships is when one partner or the other either cannot say "I'm sorry," or cannot forgive and go on. If you hold onto anger or frustration you are destined to create a feud from which there will never be a satisfactory end. You will take that anger, disappointment or hatred to the grave.

When your mate attacks you verbally, the natural reaction is to defend yourself. However, an apologetic or neutral statement can diffuse the situation and prevent an argument.

Let's examine a typical, mundane squabble that a couple might have. A wife grows upset and yells at her husband for neglecting to help with the household chores. The man feels threatened and immediately launches a verbal counter attack before objectively thinking about her complaints. The woman's initial irritation turns to outright anger upon hearing her man's verbal barbs. Before either party has had a chance to truly think about the issues at hand, a full scale fight erupts.

But let's back track for a moment. All of this conflict could have been avoided if either the husband or the wife hadn't been so venomous in their opening comments. Furthermore, instead of seeking a peaceful resolution to the argument after it had begun, each instead entered into a bitter contest of verbal snipes and jabs. The best response to a complaining mate is to honestly asses their grievances. Be open to constructive criticism, and never be too proud to say you're sorry. You will find that these two simple words neutralize more conflicts then any other phrase known to man.

If a relationship is going to succeed over the long haul, collectively the couple must develop the ability to find solutions to problems. The virtues of compromise and forgiveness need to be cultivated as well. Without these elements, you'll never truly be able to kiss and make up.

Cardinal Rule

> Always remember that a good relationship is a two-way street. No one is without fault. Compromise is the key that unlocks happiness.

Keep in mind that you do not want to exert extreme pressure on your partner to do things that are not within their comfort levels. Compromising is about both parties feeling comfortable and secure. It's important that the amount of compromise is equal on both sides. One partner shouldn't have to constantly prove their devotion by always giving in. Keep these things in mind when you have problems, and they will help to guide you through to a good solution.

STEP 15—Your Own Space

This step is many times overlooked by people in a relationship. Each partner must have space and time to themselves. The private space may be a closet, a room or a desk. Each partner should have an agenda of things that they want to accomplish and each should have the time to work towards achieving those goals. Developing a good sexual relationship does not mean that one partner must do or like everything that the other partner does or likes, or that one partner completely depends on the other for all of their activities. In a strong relationship, each person maintains an independence of thought and feeling. Each partner must respect the other's viewpoints and comments. You never want your lover to feel that the relationship is constricting and only goes one way. A supportive atmosphere should be maintained in order to allow for individual development. Personal growth can often lead to a stronger and more confident partner, one able to bring more love and support to the relationship as a whole.

Cardinal Rule

Respect each other's space and your bond will become stronger.

STEP 16—Trust

It is important in the beginning of a relationship to keep your eyes and heart open while extending trust to your new partner. Never start a relationship by comparing your new partner to a prior lover or by requiring that they to prove themselves to you.

Cardinal Rule

> If you have a pessimistic outlook regarding trust, you are destined to find yourself the victim of constant self-fulfilling prophecies.

Once a person is disappointed, it is difficult to find the courage to trust again. However, it is a key element in developing a good sexual relationship. You must have a firm foundation based on the cornerstones of honesty and trust. Give a new partner the benefit of the doubt. Trust them, and make sure to be honest in return. Only in this way will you be able to work on the other steps and elements in a relationship. Without trust and honesty, you will never attain true intimacy.

STEP 17—Make Your Partner A Friend

In a sexual relationship, it is very important to make your partner your best friend. When you're not feeling well, when you have moods, when you have desires, confide in your partner. Let them know the different sides of your personality. This way you both can become closer and more intimate.

Cardinal Rule

> Everything is nicer when shared with a special friend.

You can establish this friendship by sharing your past and your present happenings, telling him or her the likes and dislikes that you have regarding music, food, sporting events, etc. Be able to laugh at yourself and at your partner. Share the goofy as well as the serious times. When little or unimportant difficulties occur, be able to see the lighter side of the situation. If something causes you or your partner to become embarrassed, look for the humor in it. Have them relax. It's just a passing moment. Learn to comfort your partner just like you would your best friend. Confide your deepest feelings in them, and always make sure to be there for them in return.

Cardinal Rule

> Find your own safe place where you and your friend feel cozy, secure and comfortable. Then you can discuss intimately your feelings, desires and plans.

STEP 18—Affection

We all find it appealing to be involved with a partner who can show affection. You must let yourself be free and comfortable. Be able to show affection. Don't be afraid to snuggle. Hold a hand at the right time. Plant a little kiss on the cheek. Playfully wrestle your partner. Come up behind them and give them a surprise hug. Leave them notes, a flower or a surprise gift. Mail them a card.

Always make sure to keep in touch with that someone special. Give them a call at work or home, if for nothing more than to say, "I miss you, I'm thinking about you, I need you, I love you." This can really make people feel exhilarated and add some sunshine to their day.

Cardinal Rule

> Put humor in your daily life, make time to do fun things together.

STEP 19—Appearance

Appearance is usually the first thing that attracts one person to another. However, it's also the weakest link for keeping two people together in a long term relationship.

Do not confuse appearance with style or wealth. Style is usually someone else's perception of what looks good. What others feel is fashionable may not necessarily be attractive on you. Many think that simply buying expensive clothes and accessories guarantees an appealing appearance. However, it's just as easy for someone to look attractive on a very modest budget as it is for someone with a lot of money. At any rate, often expensive things look awkward or even down right unattractive.

Many in our society are preconditioned by our environment. The clothing we wear is a reflection of that. There are two common mistakes that most people make when planning a wardrobe and deciding what to wear. First, they let fashion designers dictate what they should wear. Many times this apparel will not compliment the person's physical makeup or coloring. In the case of accessories, like women's shoes, fashion apparel can even cause physical discomfort and harm. Sadly, most in today's society allow their peers to influence their choice of dress rather than picking out what suits their particular needs.

For example, think back to 1980 or so. Would the high school or college students of that era even consider wearing workman's coveralls, pants that were three sizes too big or shirts so huge that they would hang down over their knees? Back then teenagers would run screaming at the thought of wearing such clothes. Yet today on high school and college campuses across the nation this is considered in fashion. These same young adults will pay substantially higher prices for articles that have a certain logo or brand name, even though the quality of such garments often leaves a lot to be desired.

Designers need to feed both their pocketbooks and their egos and therefore they are under pressure to meet seasonal demands to change the style of something in order to make it chic. Although designers over the years have been responsible for some very positive changes in apparel, most of the changes usually are not flattering and are short lived. You have to be able to focus on what is truly good quality, and what makes you, the individual, look attractive.

Be honest with yourself, look at your wardrobe and find those things that really look appropriate and attractive on you regardless of what your friends and peers may first say. The real truth is **our appearance makes a great impact on how we are treated socially.** People who have a nice appearance and look successful receive preferential treatment in almost all levels of social life as well as in the corporate business world. This fact has been proven in many research studies.

The same point has been dramatically proven time and time again by the entertainment and movie industry. A woman dressed in sweat pants and a pullover might not draw much attention, but put that same woman in a mini-skirt and a halter top and she'll cause heads to turn. Next time you're at your newsstand or grocery store, take a moment to check out the women's and social magazines. You'll never see a woman dressed in an old T shirt and sweat pants on their covers.

The key is to be able to pick the appropriate patterns, colors and textures that will accent your appearance and will enable you to look attractive for all occasions. This can be done quite inexpensively if one shops intelligently.

There are only basically two reasons to dress: to protect yourself from the elements and to look good for the people you are meeting. Clothing can affect the way you feel about yourself. A nice outfit always pumps up one's ego.

Being attractively dressed and well-groomed will boost your ego. The subsequent increase in self confidence can help to overcome the nervous tension of social occasions or of meeting someone new. More importantly, being properly groomed and maintained will have a significant effect upon the people you meet, especially if it's that one special person.

Everyone always notices a nicely groomed person. Appearance is important because it gives you self confidence. It shows you care. We are attracted to each other by our looks. Appearances can start the chemistry between people. It may be a hair cut that first draws your attention to a person, or perhaps some eccentricity of style that they incorporate into their fashion. If advertising firms pay huge fees to have good looking, well groomed people in nice attire stand next to their product to attract attention, should you do any less when you're trying to attract someone?

STEP 20—Learn to Confide

While going through the steps of emotional development for a sexual relationship, you should come to a point when you feel secure enough to confide in your partner. Look at what the relationship is and what you would like it to be. Discuss with your partner the things that are good about it and those things that you wish to change. You must be free to express yourself and able to explain the type of affection you want inside and outside of the bedroom. Do you want more passion in your lovemaking? Would it help to have incense, candles or music? Focus on being able to voice your feelings and your opinions. This is a good thing. Discussing sex in a relationship can be difficult. Some people are not comfortable talking about their emotions.

Cardinal Rule

> Truth in communication is very important because a lack of affection or desire can affect your partner's ego. You don't want your partner to feel rejected because you were too anxious or nervous to speak the truth.

Finally, we must take the time to be intimate and truthful with ourselves and then to be intimate and truthful with our partner. Only through this will we be able to experience the true satisfaction of knowing and pleasing our partner and thus experiencing the true pleasures of a wholesome, sexual relationship. Only honest, positive, emotional intimacy will enable us to develop the type of relationship that we are seeking. Sometimes people that have physical intimacy substitute their sex drive for the need for emotional intimacy because they are guarding their emotions and are afraid or unable to reveal their feelings to their partner. In order to nurture intimacy, you must allow your heart to guide you. Express your true feelings and become emotionally, as well as physically intimate with your partner. If you feel that you don't know the person well enough to discuss such things, or don't feel comfortable to discuss these things with your partner, then you have to ask yourself the question: Should I really be developing a sexual relationship with someone I can't talk to about sex or emotions?

STEP 21—Safe Sex

Too much information has been made available for you to be irresponsible about sex. If you are not concerned about your safety regarding a sexual relationship, then you are not prepared to enter into one. A concerned, intelligent and caring person will insist on safe sex until it's known beyond a shadow of a doubt that each partner is healthy and free from any STDs. Your decision to enter into a sexual relationship will affect not only yourself, but potentially your partner, your friends and your family as well. The two key words to keep in mind when making a decision are "respect" and "responsibility." Respect yourself and your body, and take responsibility for your own actions.

There are thousands of wrong reasons for entering into a sexual relationship. However, as we have discussed and try to convey in this book, you must be both emotionally and physically prepared. Think things through clearly, so that you don't feel uncomfortable and that when you get into a sexual relationship, it will be a good experience that will make you feel happy and whole. You must consider the potential lifelong effects of having sex. You can have an unwanted pregnancy, develop emotional problems, or contract a health or life threatening disease, such as AIDS.

Cardinal Rule

Safe sex is important to a relationship because it creates confidence and trust between the partners by reaffirming each other's value of self.

Abstinence from sexual intercourse is the only foolproof way of preventing unwanted pregnancies and sexually transmitted diseases. However, the medical field does make a difference between dangerous unprotected sex and the concept of safe sex. Having safe sex is the only way to protect yourself against sexually transmitted diseases, which are very contagious. Having sexual intercourse even one time with someone who is infected can expose a person to sexually transmitted disease. These diseases can cause sterility, genital pain, irritation, nervous disorders and even death.

Cardinal Rule

> When you become involved with a new lover, you must always practice safe sex until both of you have had a complete medical exam and blood tests for STDs. As a show of good faith show your test results and make sure you see 'your partner' results. *Never* take someone's verbal statement of good health. If your lover refuses to show their test results, then either stop the relationship or have *only* protected sex.

Simple and Safe

Unfortunately, condoms have never had a good position in our society. They were "those things" you used to guard against pregnancy. However, because of the increased public awareness of sexually transmitted diseases in general and AIDS in particular, they are now in style and the safest and most preferred way to have safe sex.

A large number of medical studies have shown that latex condoms, especially if coupled with a spermicide, can dramatically reduce the chances of becoming infected with an STD. This is not to say that condoms are guaranteed to be 100% effective. They cannot completely eliminate the risk of contracting an STD or of preventing a pregnancy. Nevertheless they are the recommended and preferred method. These products are widely available, and in some cases freely given out. There is no reason for anyone to have unprotected sex.

The most important rule regarding condoms is to put the condom on before the penis comes in contact with the vagina. Most people don't This is sufficient to cause both pregnancy and the contraction of a sexually transmitted disease. Place the correct side of the condom against the head of the penis and unroll it all the way down to the base of the penis (if the condom does not unroll easily, you have it backwards). Pinch the tip of the condom as you roll it on, so that there is some empty space at end, preferably one half of an inch. Try not to leave a bubble of air at the tip as this may cause the condom to slip or burst.

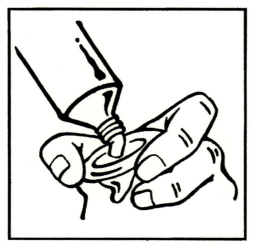

Proper technique for using spermicide with a latex condom.

The condom is very thin and is designed for protection and to give as much sensitivity as possible to both partners. The best way to penetrate the woman is to wait until she is well lubricated, or use a water-based lubricant. A non-lubricated vagina is more likely to tear the condom. Also, the sensitivity is greatly enhanced when there is a lubricant involved, resulting in more pleasure for the woman. Sometimes penetration with a dry condom or dry penis can be irritable and painful for the woman. If you use a condom during anal intercourse, be particularly careful. It is very susceptible to tearing. It is recommended that you use the proper lubricant.

After intercourse, always remove the condom and avoid spillage of its contents. Check the condom for leaks and discard it. Never reuse a condom under any circumstances. Some people believe that they can wash a condom and reuse it. This is a dangerous and erroneous belief. Used condoms have lost their sterile aspects and elasticity and are more susceptible to breakage.

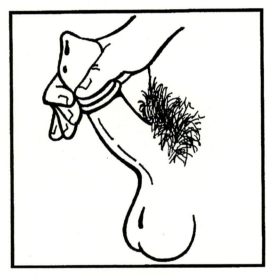

Proper technique for putting on a latex condom.

If you discover a leak, have your partner immediately apply spermicide to her vagina without delay. Do a proper washing. Medical studies have shown that even in the case of some sexually transmitted diseases, if the area is completely flushed out and washed with soap, it will destroy or remove the STD. If a condom breaks while being used to guard against pregnancy, then the woman should consult with her physician as soon as possible. You may be able to get a morning after pill which can reduce the chances of getting pregnant if taken within 72 hours of intercourse.

Special Notes Regarding Condoms

Avoid using condoms that are more than two years old. It may have deteriorated and be more prone to breakage. Store condoms in a dry place away from heat and light. Unfortunately, many people are used to carrying condoms in a purse or wallet. These are bad places to keep them for any long period of time.

Never, under any circumstances, use petroleum based lubricants, like Vaseline, with a condom. Never use vaginal medications, including Monistat, Premarin, Estrace, Vagisil or any other feminine product. These products have a chemical in them that will cause the latex condom to deteriorate, allowing the passage of sperm and microscopic organisms. We will discuss some exciting and exotic ways to put on condoms so that it can be a part of the foreplay and pleasure for both the man and the woman. Recently, researchers have developed a female product that serves as a condom. However, medical studies have shown that this device is not as trustworthy as a traditional, male worn condom. The female condom has a tendency to be pushed or moved out of place prematurely and, therefore, does not offer the protection that the traditional male condom offers.

How to Use a Condom Guide

The U.S. Department of Health and Human Services, Food and Drug Administration has set forth these guidelines regarding condom use:

- Use a new condom for every act of intercourse.
- If the penis is uncircumcised, pull the foreskin back before putting the condom on.

- Put the condom on after the penis is erect (hard) and before any contact is made between the penis and any part of the partner's body.
- If using a spermicide, put some inside the condom tip.
- If the condom does not have a reservoir tip, pinch the tip enough to leave a half-inch space for semen to collect.
- While pinching the half-inch tip, place the condom against the penis and unroll it all the way to the base. Put more spermicide or lubricant on the outside.
- If you feel a condom break while you are having sex, stop immediately and pull out. Do not continue until you have put on a new condom and used more spermicide.
- After ejaculation and before the penis gets soft, grip the rim of the condom and carefully withdraw from your partner.
- To remove the condom from the penis, pull it off gently, being careful semen doesn't spill out.
- Wrap the used condom in a tissue and throw it in the trash where others won't handle it. Because condoms may cause problems in sewers, don't flush them down the toilet. Afterwards, wash your hands with soap and water.
- Finally, be ware of drugs and alcohol! They can affect your judgment, so you may forget to use a condom. They may even affect your ability to use a condom properly.

One final note: Do not become confused by the word contraceptive. Many contraceptives are devices that are effective only in preventing pregnancies and offer absolutely no protection against AIDS or other sexually transmitted diseases. For example, diaphragms, cervical caps and contraceptive sponges all prevent pregnancy, but do little to guard against disease. The only recommended protection for both unwanted pregnancies and sexually transmitted diseases is the traditional male worn condom.

Practicing safer sex means engaging in sexual intercourse that can potentially be dangerous. However, you can drastically reduce the risk by using the proper precautions until you and your partner have had an opportunity to have a complete medical examination and know for sure that you are healthy and STD free. This will allow you to have unprotected sex if you are not concerned about the pregnancy aspect. Safer sex allows you to enjoy sexual contact without acquiring sexually transmitted diseases.

There are many different ways to broach the topic of sexually transmitted diseases with your partner. All the different methods of safer sex and how to work within your family unit regarding safer sex, are discussed in detail in book three of the *Trilogy of Sexually Relationships*. However, at this time we will say that you should always use a latex condom plus spermicide containing nonoxynol-9 when having sexual intercourse. When you start a new sexual relationship, chose your partner wisely, share sexual and medical histories and have the appropriate medical examinations done before ever having any sexual contact without a latex condom. STDs are transmitted through blood and certain other bodily fluids such as amniotic fluid, pericardial fluid, peritoneal fluid, pleural fluid, synovial fluid, cerebrospinal fluid, semen, vaginal secretions or any bodily fluid visibly contaminated with blood.

It is considered safe to kiss, massage, hug, rub or generally caress your partner.

The *Trilogy on Sexual Relationships* is not meant to take the place of sound counseling by a physician.

Many people believe that if a person wants answers to their questions on sex, they can go to their parents, family doctor or teacher. However, the reality is that most people feel uncomfortable discussing the subject.

Children rarely seek answers from their parents, the school system rarely has good programs on sex ed and many churches rely upon the family and schools for sexual education. Surveys and studies from the past decade, including ones undertaken by the Kinsey Institute and Roper National Sex Knowledge Test, demonstrate that the vast majority of people are either unaware or improperly informed regarding sexual relationships and sexually transmitted diseases.

In order to be 100% sure that you do not contract a sexually transmitted disease or become pregnant, you must refrain from sexual intercourse and remain abstinent. However, you can still enjoy a sexual relationship. You can both give and receive pleasure as we will illustrate later in the book by the use of hands and body rubbing. However, be very careful that you do not have any open cuts or sores on your hands when coming into contact with bodily fluids or the genital area.

Cardinal Rule

> Coitus interruptus, the withdrawal of the penis from the vagina just before ejaculation, is *NOT* an effective form of birth control and offers *NO* protection against STDs.

No matter how exciting a sex act is, it takes only one unprotected encounter to contract a sexually transmitted disease. No single sex act, no matter how pleasurable, is worth a lifetime of pain and discomfort.

Please refer to book three of the Trilogy for information about sexually transmitted diseases and the methods of safer sex and the enjoyment of a safer sex relationship.

STEP 22—Loyalty

Loyalty is one of the most highly appreciated characteristics that one can bring to a sexual relationship. Loyalty goes beyond honesty. It means one can depend on you in a time of need, one can rely on you in a time of crisis. It means that your partner can rely on your judgment, your feelings and your sincerity. An absence of loyalty is often the reason that so many marriages end up in divorce court.

Many of the problems that couples face during a marriage can be resolved if they have enough patience and have followed the steps to develop a good sexual relationship. Couples can use the steps to overcome most difficulties, except for problems involving loyalty. Once one has lost trust in the other partner's loyalty, usually it cannot be restored and thus the marriage or relationship is destined for difficulty or break up.

Cardinal Rule

> Our worst mistake in a relationship comes about by thinking we will be forgiven no matter what we do.

STEP 23—Sexuality and Romance

Love can move mountains, but if you do not keep the sexuality and romance in your relationship, your union will quickly become mundane. Once this happens, love won't even move somebody off the sofa. In today's society, many marriages end up in divorce court and both the man and woman, along with the children, receive many emotional scars as a result. It is very common to hear after the divorce, when people reflect, that they let their careers, interests and other things take the place of the desire and romance that was in the relationship originally, and that they put the relationship on the back burner. This soon creates wanting and frustration. As you will see when we talk about the topic, "Seduction," one of the key factors in developing love is to affirm each other's gender as well as each other's esteem and ego. Although people will make many accusations and blame one another, what has really happened when a relationship breaks up is that we've lost the capability of keeping the romance and love alive. If people are able to be honest and intimate and can keep open lines of communication and interact, then they can continue to renew their love for each other. The key is to always give emotional support. This will help both partners overcome the problems that all encounter during their relationships, while still maintaining their interest in one another.

Most men and women are looking for the same thing in a relationship. Many seek unions that will lead to children, rewarding and meaningful sex, security and commitment.

You must be able to renew the things that originally brought you together and that you found reassured each other's gender and desires. You must be able to, as they say, "not sweat the small stuff." Learn how to be able to laugh together, work together, remain non-critical, and develop honest, intimate communication. Do not let family or friends influence you wrongly in making poor or snap decisions. You have to work together on your own time schedule and in your own way to keep sexuality and romance in your relationship.

In order to accomplish this goal, you need to take time and put effort into the relationship. You each have to make a commitment to each other. Your goal is to obtain a long term, meaningful relationship. Here are some aids to help you accomplish that goal and stay on target.

- When your desires, emotions or needs aren't completely satisfied, this may trigger frustration, anger or jealously. However, do not feed upon this because it will only cause you to be more unhappy. Learn to express yourself and talk and communicate in a sincere, calm way to your mate and explain what your needs or beliefs are and see if you can work out a solution. This is very important to be able to have a good coexistence.

- It is important during a relationship to have both patience and empathy. Both men and women at times, due to anxiety, anger, illness, stress or work, may find themselves having a reduced desire for sexual intimacy and contact. If you find yourself in this situation and you feel that your partner is not as sexually active or does not desire sex as they did, do not criticize or challenge. Instead, open the lines of communication and see if you can find a solution to what is causing the problem. Women should remember that it is sometimes very difficult for men to talk about their sexual activity because they do not feel it is "macho," and it is very threatening to a man's ego because it makes them feel insecure. However, if both of you put sincere effort into finding a solution, you will find that the payoff is a passionate mate who can then be there for you when you need it.

- Do not take into your relationship a self-fulfilling prophecy that if things don't work out the way you want them, you're going to leave. Every relationship, no matter how good it is, will have problems and stress at times. It is the ones who have enough determination and compassion that can overcome the problems or find a solution. It is the ones who are quick to anger and lack self-confidence that usually have the self-fulfilling prophecy come true. They always turn and say, "well things didn't work out, that's why I left." Try to never make an important decision under extreme frustration or in a hurry. Allow yourself and your partner time to relax, think things over in a cool and calm way, and try in privacy to resolve the issues. Never allow other people to inflame the situation and make the decision for you. Do not become one of those casualties who have regrets at the end of their life for the things they wished they would have done or could have done a different way.

- To keep romance in your relationship, make a commitment to privately get together at least once a day. Allow enough time so that each of you have an opportunity to discuss things that are on your mind.

- Never be too busy for your mate. If there is a pressing problem that they have, have the understanding and empathy to take the time to listen. Even if you cannot resolve their problem, it will help to discuss and show your compassion.

- Set an agenda so that you will go out together alone, without children, family or friends, at least once every two weeks or once every month. Reunite the intimacy and romance that you had when you were first dating and wanted "private time together."

- Make a surprise phone call to your loved one at least once a week. You don't have to say much. "I love you, I miss you," or, "I'm thinking of you," will all do fine. This goes a long way to putting a little sunshine into everyone's day and to create that special bond between you and your loved one.

- Try to be playful occasionally. Don't ever loose the ability to laugh with your loved one. Use the pet names or special names of endearment that you called them when you first started the relationship. Always put the mood of romance into your relationship.

- Do something spontaneous and unusual. No matter what your age you can be sexy and alluring. Suggest taking a bath or shower together, or buy something fancy and soft. The thought is often more stimulating than the action itself, and you can put a sense of romance back into your emotions.

- It's always nice to receive a card or letter in the mail or a little surprise gift. It doesn't have to be expensive, just cute and unusual. Do something simple like leaving a rose on the pillow in the morning or bring home a bag of popcorn and wine and ask your spouse to watch a movie alone with you.
- Plan on having a late candle light dinner one night after the children are in bed.
- Touching is so powerful. Suggest a nice oil rub or massage and see where that leads.
- You women can drive your men crazy by putting a sexy note in either his briefcase or his lunch. See how long it takes him to get home that night. Promise him an evening he'll never forget. For you men, if you have children, surprise her by making arrangements for a babysitter to take care of the children and take her out unexpectedly for the evening. Or better yet, plan a special rendezvous at a hotel for the evening.
- Work, children, illness, exhaustion, stress and anxiety can put a terrible burden on any relationship and can diminish the sex drive that you have for each other. When love is wanting and one partner seems to be drifting, the doctor's remedy is a special interlude, a change, a vacation, a time by yourself away from the pressures. An opportunity to reunite the intimacy and care is a wonderful cure and tremendous energy boost. Nothing will help your romance more than re-igniting the fire in your relationship. You should take the care to plan a special interlude at least several times a year in order to regenerate yourself and your relationship.

Cardinal Rule

> Your daily lives will create many obstacles and excuses for not spending time together and being romantic. However, romance can be the source of energy, inspiration and love. The key to a good romance is to prioritize. Your relationship and your happiness should come first. Make sure you put aside the time for that priority.

No one ever outgrows the need for sexuality in their relationship. It is sad but true that many people today give reasons or excuses—they are too tired, they want to wait until the children grow up and leave. The career or job is too important. The duties as a mother are overwhelming. There is not enough time in the day. All these things remove the sexuality and romance out of a relationship if you allow them to. However, you must be able to focus and give your undivided attention to your mate. In order to keep a relationship vibrant, it is not just the sexual bonds, it is the sharing of time, the intimacy, the communication, the ability to have time to yourselves, to focus on your needs, desires, dreams and feelings. Therefore, this time is the most essential and you should plan it into your schedule. Although this may be a challenge at times, it is essential for lovers to have this time in order to rejuvenate their bond.

Cardinal Rule

> It's the thought that counts. A romantic setting with a beer and hot dog can create a romantic mood just as well as wine, crystal and lobster.

It is more difficult for two people to maintain a high degree of love and intimacy over the course of many years. This is especially true in a family unit where the children are always needing attention. However, you must consciously put in the effort to keep in your relationship the sexuality, the intimacy, the honesty and spontaneity in order to keep the romance alive.

Most people will be very surprised when they realize how much additional energy and fun they can have when they keep the sexuality and romance alive in their relationship. It has a way of removing the anxiety and stress of every day living. When people forget to make the effort to keep romance and sexuality alive in their relationship, that is the point they start to grow apart and the relationship begins to fade.

Cardinal Rule

> Excuses and results are mutually exclusive—if you have one—you don't have the other. Always make time for romance.

People change as they grow, not only individuals but within a relationship. This is natural. If you are honest and put forth the effort and communicate to your partner the change can be positive and make the bonds grow even stronger in the relationship. If you continue to review the 24 steps in building a relationship and renew the self-esteem and your love, you will know how to handle problems, you will be able to fix things when it is necessary. You will show empathy and the two of you can grow happy because you are helping each other and you will find that this can be very exhilarating and pleasurable. You will be able to build a trust in your relationship that will give you the energy to get through each day and you will continue to build a solid foundation which will nurture your love and relationship.

Cardinal Rule

> A long term successful relationship is the ability to continue to fall in love with the same person again and again in new ways.

In today's society with both the man and woman working while trying to raise a family and continue the relationship, many couples have experienced that romance dies in a long term relationship and marriage.

Raising children, careers, obligations, one thing after another, seems to take each other's time and energy and before they know it, the passionate love they had in the relationship has started to fade and erode. If you let this happen, you are allowing the priorities in your life to become out of balance. You have allowed other items to rob you of your precious time and energy. You must take control of your life and the happiness and love you want—not tomorrow—but today. You cannot put the most important priority in your life, which is your happiness and your relationship and your family unit to second or third place. You must make the effort to practice the techniques that we discussed in this chapter about rekindling the sexuality and romance in your relationship. Do not look for excuses, do not blame it on things like if I were thinner, or if I had more money, or if I had a bigger house or a better job. If you do that it will never happen. You will always be waiting and your relationship will continue to erode and fade. Your relationship, your life, your marriage, is the number one priority and you must take care of your number one priority. Use the techniques that we discussed in this section to put the relationship back on track, to put the sexuality and romance back into your life. Bring back the little courtship rituals that you used when you first started dating. Try to take and include each other in small ways into each others lives on a daily basis. Think of all the reasons why you love each other and share them with each other. In doing this you will strengthen your relationship, put a new energy and exhilaration into yourself and revitalize the love and energy in your relationship.

Cardinal Rule

Falling in love is easy, staying in love takes effort and romance.

STEP 24—Personal Hygiene, Know Your Body

Personal hygiene is as important as physical appearance in developing a sexual relationship. Nothing can kill a romantic mood quicker than bad breath. Over a period of time even the strongest attraction to a partner will have difficulty overcoming bad personal hygiene.

Even more important, each of us should be responsible for doing self-examinations regularly while bathing in order to look for any changes or symptoms. This is important for everyone, not just sexually active people. Everyone should always properly shampoo their hair and bathe. Brush your teeth and use antiseptic mouthwash. Carry breath mints or spray with you. Women should be careful not to use too much makeup or lipstick. This factor can also be a real turn off to certain men. Both men and women should be aware of the cologne and cosmetics that they use, as it can be an irritant to their partner, causing a rash or an allergic reaction. It is always best to check first.

Taking time to properly groom is important. It gives one a good feeling about themselves and is a real ego builder. At the same time, it avoids the problem of being a real turn off to someone that you are meeting. It is difficult to develop a relationship if the first impression one makes is a negative one because they are not properly groomed or they are not using proper hygiene.

Women should understand their anatomy and learn to recognize signs of problems early, especially during the reproductive cycle.

Every man and woman must take responsibility for monitoring their own health and also be aware of the symptoms of sexually transmitted diseases. Always schedule a medical examination whenever changes or symptoms of a problem are noticed.

Always use safe sex techniques. It takes only one unprotected encounter to contract a sexually transmitted disease and no single sex act is worth a life of pain or discomfort or even your life itself.

Female Sexual Hygiene

Women, because of their special internal reproductive anatomy should pay special attention to their menstrual cycle. Physicians recommend that from the age of puberty you should keep a record of when you have your menstrual cycle. It can be invaluable for diagnosing many different types of problems and is much more accurate then vague recollections when you are talking to a doctor about changes in your cycle. The average length between one menstrual flow and the next is 28 days. However, cycle lengths vary from one woman to another. As a woman goes from puberty to menopause she can have tremendous variations in her cycle and amount of menstrual flow. Sometimes while a woman is maturing the periods may vary in timing, amount and color. All of this can be natural and should not be alarming. However, it is important to be aware of your menstrual cycle when you are discussing problems with your physician. The changes may be symptoms of something that needs treatment.

The female external genitals should be periodically examined. If any change takes place, you should contact your physician immediately. Just below the clitoris is a very small urinary opening. Below that is the vaginal opening. Because these openings are so close to each other, many women experience urinary infections after having sex.

Just below the vaginal opening and where the labia meet is a small area of smooth, usually hairless, skin. Below that is the anus. Women should always be careful to wipe from the front to the back after using the toilet to avoid having fecal matter transferred near the vaginal and urinary openings. This can be a common cause of vaginal and uterine infections.

Keep yourself physically fit and sexually active and you can go on enjoying satisfying and pleasurable sex almost to the very end of your life. A 72-year old woman told researchers Bernard Starr, Ph.D., and Marcella Weintar, Ed.D., "Our sex is so much more relaxed I know my body better, and we know each other better. Sex is unhurried and the *best* in our lives."

Tips to Stay Healthy

The U.S. Department of Health and Human Services recommends following these general guidelines:

- Eat a balanced diet
- Get plenty of rest
- Exercise regularly
- Avoid infections
- Learn to relax and deal with stress
- Do not take unnecessary medications—especially antibiotics and steroids
- Practice safe sex
- Do not use drugs like marijuana, speed, cocaine, downers, nicotine or heroin

Cardinal Rule

A healthy body increases the pleasure of sex. Sexual activity can rejuvenate the body and you alone have control over one of the greatest ways to pleasure yourself. Use this control wisely and prudently.

Chapter IV

What Destroys Relationships—Avoid The Pitfalls

The following forms of thinking are negative and distorted and can cause a great deal of anxiety in developing a wholesome sexual relationship. The information in this book is the result of numerous interviews, discussions and support groups. Each of the following descriptions includes an explanation of how this topic can challenge or cause confusion in developing a wholesome sexual relationship.

Former Sexual Relationships

Although honesty is a key fundamental block in building a good sexual relationship, from interviews with support groups we have learned that in almost all cases, discussing former sexual relationships will create distrust, anxiety between the parties and frustration. It hinders a romance from developing. Some may think that boasting about former sexual relationships and activities increases their desirability. In fact, it can have the exact opposite effect. Some people will even emotionally hurt themselves because subconsciously this will lower their self esteem. So unless there is something positive to be gained, a discussion of your prior sexual relationships should never be discussed when developing a new relationship.

Labeling and Over-Generalization

Using a label to describe your partner or over-generalizing about certain traits of theirs can cause adverse affects. We are not discussing words of endearment. We are talking about the derogatory labels that people will sometimes use in a relationship or the over-generalizations of certain activities that should be kept intimate. Sometimes we rush in what we're saying and we fail to understand our true emotions. Using labels when discussing activities or personality traits can cause a great deal of anxiety, self pity or frustration. The end result is that it will act negatively upon developing a wholesome and rewarding sexual relationship.

Realize that some people can be very innocent and immature when it comes to the art of a sexual relationship. They should not be ridiculed or questioned, but encouraged so they feel comfortable and competent and emotionally able to handle the relationship. One should find ego-strengtheners so that you encourage and reaffirm the positive in a relationship. Doing this will pay big rewards in the long term.

The thing to keep in mind is that in the process of overcoming a social anxiety, people experience moderate amounts of frustration and fear and they will react to the comments and labels that someone puts on them. Saying, "you're dumb if you don't understand this," or "you're dumb if you don't like this," can seriously damage a person's view of themselves. Subconsciously they will think, "well I'm either bad at this or wrong," when in reality there is no truth to the statement. So avoid making your partner feel uncomfortable and allow them to develop their own feelings and expressions and enjoy the relationship without creating anxiety by using negative labels or over-generalizations of what they should feel or do, or how they should react.

Discussing the Ex

There is very little merit in discussing one's ex-boyfriend, ex-girlfriend or ex-spouse. From research we have found that in most cases it will create anxiety and hang-ups in developing a long-term sexual relationship. In fact, case studies show that it may even cause the break up and disintegration of a good sexual relationship. The discussion about an ex causes a great deal of negative thought. Are people being compared and being put up to a standard? Is that person still emotionally and sexually involved with the ex? Is that person so desirous of the ex that they cannot focus on a new relationship? Will that person be able to leave the prior relationship and ex in the past and develop a new life? Unless the discussion of an ex has a constructive positive purpose, refrain from talking about them. Usually discussing past events, exploits and appearances of the ex only causes doubts in your new partner's mind.

Secrets

Keeping secrets or having your partner keep a secret for you is a major cause for fear and anxiety problems to develop and is a major road block in developing a good sexual relationship. Maintaining good communications between the partners is essential in developing a good sexual relationship. Therefore, do not place a burden upon the development of your relationship by keeping a major secret from your partner that would adversely affect your relationship, or by making your relationship conditional upon keeping a secret. This is especially true when the secret is kept from the parents or the children of the partner. This puts such a tremendous burden on the relationship that many times the partner will never feel at ease and comfortable in a sexual relationship. Situations should be discussed amongst the partners so that they can overcome their anxiety related to the reason of the secret, and then they need to learn how to manage the problem or the secret. In some cases involving more complex factors, the secret may make a meaningful sexual relationship unattainable and impossible.

Cardinal Rule

> Keeping a secret often causes a situation to get worse and puts pressure on your relationship.

Friends and Family

If you are embarrassed about having your partner meet your friends or family, then unconsciously you are telling your partner that they are not good enough in your eyes. It also implies that you don't trust your own judgement and that you have made bad moves in your relationships before. If you have these feelings, discuss them, cope with them, resolve them. If you cannot bring yourself to feeling comfortable and fond of your partner, then you will not be able to develop a good and meaningful sexual relationship. Having mutual respect and admiration for each other is another cornerstone in a good relationship.

Never tell your partner that you are ashamed of them. If you are, and if you say this, it will almost certainly create a great deal of anxiety and reluctancy in your partner and soon mistrust and anger will come into play and make it very difficult for anyone to overcome these feelings.

Being Superficial

Be careful in using words of endearment or of proclaiming love too soon in a relationship. First, it is possible that you can create anxiety in your partner by thinking things are beyond the point that they are. Things may be moving too fast for your partner, and they may require more time to feel the same way as you do. Getting too emotional too quickly can cause you to stumble in developing a good sexual relationship. Also, using words of endearment or saying, "I love you," too soon in a relationship can make the other person feel that you are casual or shallow, and not really in control of your true feelings and emotions. This in turn can make them feel that you're not prepared to enter into a meaningful sexual relationship. Don't rush yourself. When the time feels right and you know for certain your feelings, then be open and free. Then use "I love you," in a meaningful and proper way.

Careers

Do not make the mistake of mixing your sexual relationships with your career. Do not showcase your partner as an object of conquest. This can many times cause severe anxiety problems. The partner is put in a position of having the tough responsibility of constantly being "on stage" and this causes a great deal of anxiety and resentment at times. It also can create a feeling of being under-appreciated and used. A partner may spend years trying to be acceptable and pleasing to somebody else's standards or ideals. This is not what a good sexual relationship is about. This also means that one should not, unless it's been agreed upon by both partners, discuss a sexual relationship in a career or social atmosphere. This can also make a person tense and unhappy and uncomfortable and will eventually lead to resentment and anxiety because they will feel that they're on trial, that they are being tested and compared, and they have to give a special performance. All of this can trigger increased anxiety and frustration and create problems in a sexual relationship.

Lies

A good relationship can never be based upon lies. We are not talking about an innocent fib like, "yes you look good in that dress," or, "you look handsome in that suit." We are talking about the lies that cause self deceptions, usually in the form of unexamined attitudes, feelings or beliefs meant to protect us from our anxieties about sex and intimacy. But instead of keeping us safe they perpetuate fear and discomfort, preventing us from experiencing real pleasure and satisfaction. The lies take two forms. Lies we tell ourselves, like, "we must be having good sex, my partner is happy and satisfied although I'm not feeling anything and I haven't experienced an orgasm," or the lies we tell each other, like, "sexual relationship and sexual pleasure don't matter to me. As long as you're happy, I'm okay." When this happens, what we are really doing is trying to overcome our feelings of anxiety and fear and avoiding addressing our true feelings. Women more than men have a tendency to conceal and hide their feelings and lie about the relationship. They will usually put up with more and forgive more. They will many times try to convince themselves that their own needs are minimal and that they get pleasure out of giving pleasure. However, all of this makes a weak foundation for a good sexual relationship. A woman may honestly feel, or make herself believe, that during sexual encounters an orgasm isn't critical. However, sex without satisfaction and excitement will only lead to a weak relationship. Most of the time, women talk themselves into the thought because they are under pressure from the anxiety of keeping up with the partner's concept of what a sexual involvement should be. Some partners have a great deal of anxiety over intercourse, and as a result lie to themselves that sexual pleasure doesn't matter and a sexual relationship doesn't matter, rather than directly addressing the feelings of why they have these fears and anxieties. The anxiety and fear over sex can be shared just as easily by men as women. Many times people are scared to become involved and feel inadequate and unsure of themselves. They feel that it is a concept that's beyond them.

Most times they just have to stop telling themselves lies and learn to relax, take some risks, and be willing to experiment to find the right things that create pleasure for both partners.

Some of the other areas of lies that we tell each other or ourselves are that, "if I had a better body I would have better sex. If I use some form of stimulant or drug that my performance would be better." Sometimes, because people are fond of someone, they are not sure how to communicate and hold back their real desires because they don't want to hurt their partner's feelings. If you fall into these lies and lack the self confidence to communicate your feelings to your partner, then these lies will become self fulfilling, and you will not be able to make your sexual relationship better. You will not be gratified by the act of intimacy and sex. In order to make your relationship better, you must be able to be direct, honest and express your desires as well as your fears, and be able to take some risks and open up to your partner. Then you will be able to have true intimacy and pleasure in your relationship.

Remember, sex will only get better if you take steps to make it better.

Religion

Discussing religious viewpoints and opinions is a matter that has to be handled in a careful way. If you criticize one's religious beliefs or viewpoints, you will alienate that person and cause them to become apprehensive and fearful of a relationship. You must be able to be mature enough to avoid making allegations or assumptions and sensitive enough that you can understand and appreciate the other person's viewpoint and feelings. Never try to discuss religious viewpoints in the heat of passion, but in a relaxed and calm manner without trying to hurt or reject someone's feelings and beliefs. Ask questions and bring out the facts that have to be discussed regarding changing one's feelings or viewpoints. Different religions have different laws regarding intimacy and sex. The couple's sex relationship can only get better if they are able to understand, accept, respect and work within the framework of their beliefs. Otherwise, the relationship will develop problems and you will never be able to obtain true intimacy if one or the other partner has feelings of fear, sacrificing, self-deception or guilt.

It will surprise many that when you discuss the different feelings and beliefs you have in religion, that many of the beliefs are very compatible. Differences regarding issues can be resolved without anger and frustration, thus laying the groundwork for a peaceful sexual relationship.

Cardinal Rule

Be careful to avoid the major reasons relationships and marriages fail. Interfering relatives, excessive criticism or a lack of communication can cause financial, emotional and sexual problems.

Chapter V

Chemistry of a Sexual Relationship

Love At First Sight

Some humans seem to be programmed somewhat like mating animals and are able to fall in love at first sight. No one has been able to clearly explain why and how this happens to some people and not to others. However, the one key ingredient in falling in love at first sight seems to be timing. The timing is everything. Both people must be prepared and willing to enter into a sexual relationship and be attracted to each other instantly. The attraction is created by the sum of a person's style, body odor, pheromones, personality and love characteristics. All of the traits that we've outlined earlier come into play and match or compliment each other.

Often, the most attractive traits are ones that we cannot define or control. Perhaps you remind someone of a loving parent, or your laugh reminds them of a cherished childhood companion. From experience, we have found that many times it's characteristics like these that cause the first sparks of attraction. The meeting can be magical or mysterious. It can even be exasperating. However, if all the chemistry is right and if the timing is right, things will happen and you will get a rush of instant emotion. So understand it, enjoy it and go with it.

Sensation of Smell

Your personal scent, your pheromones, is your own individual calling card. When two people meet, that very first instant, after being attracted by the appearance of the opposite sex, the next key ingredient is scent.

None of the research foundations have been able to explain why scent can influence each of us or how much it actually affects us. For each person it is different. That first scent of the body aroma or of a cologne or perfume may produce a powerful attraction and mating call or it can be a quick turn off. All that the doctors and research groups can tell us is that it is an influence and that the first impression one receives can guide us in a direction of either an enchanting relationship or a quick turn off.

It appears that both men and women's noses are still very much drawn to each other's scent and colognes. Studies from different institutions show that certain scents have more appealing or attractive powers. Lavender, spices and wood are among the many fragrances that fall into this category. Recent studies have shown that humans may have sexual pheromones that attract each other. If this is the case, then a sprits of cologne here and there can work magic in attracting the right person. After all, the pheromones were detected in animals long ago and researchers today are saying that people like animals can sniff out each other's acute sex odor. However, if this is true, then although there are many perfumes and scents on the market today, the ultimate sex scent is your own natural odor.

Chapter VI

How to Increase Your Sex Drive

Aphrodisiacs—Love Food

People have sought out aphrodisiacs or love foods since time began. The ancient Greeks had their own secret formulas to enhance romantic and sexual interludes. Aphrodisiacs can amplify an ordinary sexual experience into something sensational and mystic. Just the thought and mental emotion that can be conjured up can cause additional excitement and pleasure. The physical act of sharing food and eating together itself can be romantic and sexually stimulating.

Some of the aphrodisiacs are based upon ancient legends and myths. Some have been examined, studied and verified by medical studies, while others are simply old folk lore and have no truth to them at all. The real test is in the experimentation and how we each react to the stimulant and in some cases the suggestion surrounding the stimulant.

This section is a collection of information about love potions and aphrodisiacs. It has been put into the form of a guide with some suggestions on appropriate or fun uses.

Never ever confuse harmful drugs with aphrodisiacs. Marijuana and cocaine have many false myths, especially regarding sexual pleasures. In truth, both these drugs can sabotage testosterone function and diminish your sexual drive and pleasure. In some severe cases they can even prevent or reduce a person's ability to maintain erections. Another dangerous substance often mistaken for an aphrodisiac is GHB, also known as the date rape drug. This is a harmful and illegal drug that should not be used for sexual pleasures. Another is the Spanish Fly. This drug, although it may rush blood to the sex organs, does it in a improper manner because it causes irritation to the urogenital track because of its components of beetle parts. It can also singe the throat and trigger genitourinary infections, scar the urethra, and in some cases has been known to kill people. Finally, there's Viagra. Viagra is a drug prescribed for those who have problems with impotence, and is designed to help the flow of blood and maintain proper erections. However, unless medically prescribed and used properly, Viagra can cause certain side effects and can be harmful to one's health, especially if they have diabetes or heart problems.

The passion and pleasure that you seek in a relationship can be obtained without resorting to the use of foreign substances and drugs. You will gain greater benefits and pleasures when you use your own natural talents and a positive ego.

The aphrodisiac that is extremely versatile and enjoyable is chocolate because cocoa contains PEA (phenylethylamine), the same endorphin that moves into the blood stream when you fall in love. It is also sensuous to have someone put chocolate covered strawberries or chocolate covered fruit from their lips to yours. The emotional turn on can be as great as the physical turn on. There are so many sensuous things you can do with chocolate. Licking or kissing chocolate off of your partner's body can be a sensuous and enjoyable experience for both partners. Just the thought can bring about very sensuous thoughts and pleasures.

According to legend, bee pollen honey is supposed to put you into a calm mood and prepare you for a sexual relationship. Usually two or three teaspoons is sufficient.

Zinc helps manufacture testosterone in both sexes. Oysters and certain seafoods are especially rich and therefore considered an aphrodisiac, especially for staying power. Niacin (Vitamin B3) is essential because it helps dilate blood vessels. One of the benefits of this is it causes the genitals to blush and the rest of you to tingle. This essential nutrient is found in things like avocados, asparagus, peanuts, figs, and especially fish. You can almost prepare an aphrodisiac feast around some of these items.

Damiana (Turnera diffusa) can be obtained in capsule, tonic or tea. The plant's leaf and stem possess a chemical that is a nerve stimulant that sets male and female genitals tingling and you can receive soothing vibrations. However, the effects are gradual and take time to manifest. The easiest way to gain this effect is to get some Damiana leaves and make a pot of tea.

Among Asian men there has been a myth that emu egg shells are an aphrodisiac and can heighten sexual enjoyment. The shells are crushed into a fine powder that is bought and sold by the gram. The shells are very similar to egg shells so you are really buying an egg shell powder and then using it in either a drink or food. There is no medical support for this legend.

For thousands of years the extract from a tree called Ginkgo Biloba has been used in medicine to help circulate blood throughout the body. You can purchase this extract in a pill form from health stores. It is said that it helps the vascular system, which in turn increases the flow of blood to the penis. This results in prolonged erections. Also, this can help grant additional sensitivity and stimulation to the penis.

The Asian use of Panax Ginseng boosts energy and vitality and thus can make both sexes overwhelmingly potent, giving the person a full adrenalin rush. Supposedly, use of this type of ginseng can help make one feel exhilarated and increase the sensitivity and performance in a sexual relationship.

Kava Kava is alleged to produce a calming high, relax the muscles and relieve anxiety regarding sexual contact. This vegetable is a member of the pepper family. It is available in health food stores in capsule form. It is all natural and it is said that it works in a very short time, usually within one or two hours. Sometimes this aphrodisiac can be of great benefit to people who suffer from anxiety and are having a difficult time performing or enjoying a sexual relationship.

Cardinal Rule

The proper aphrodisiac can increase the life force, give a vitamin boost and increase the pleasure of sex. Each person is different and each person has different needs. You must find out what improves your health and sex.

L-arginine can help to release nitric oxide, a neuro transmitter that may help the penis maintain a solid erection. It is a form of amino acid and this ingredient can be found in many dairy products, meats, nuts, and in our old friend chocolate. This ingredient is like a natural Viagra and can produce some of the same results. Look on the labels to find out what items are rich in this amino acid.

South American folk lore says that a love potion that can cure impotency is Marapuama tea (a.k.a. muirapuama). If taken, this tea supposedly can heighten one's sex drive, generating a real urge. However, we have been unable to verify this through any medical research.

James Goldberg M.D., a specialist and co-author of sexual pharmacology, states that DHEA can give both men and women benefits similar to those of testosterone, namely a subliminal urge to get it on (it also promotes longevity overall). DHEA is a mild androgen, a form of a male sex hormone. Testosterone is available by prescription only and should be used under medical supervision. However, it has been hailed as being able to pump up one's sex drive in both men and women. It is an especially strong aphrodisiac for women. However, use of this is only advised in those cases where there may be a chemical imbalance and people will need this additional testosterone to bring them up to a good performance level.

Some doctors may recommend the herb yohimbine for the treatment of impotency. The benefit of the herb is that it creates a driving force of blood to the erectile tissues, thereby producing a solid, very hard and sustained erection.

Finally, there is the nectar of Greek gods, wine. The alcohol in the wine dilates your blood vessels causing your genitals to blush and even makes your most agitated person feel calm and mellow. Thus the moderate use of wine can be beneficial in relaxing and putting one into a pleasant state for a sexual relationship.

I have listed the different ingredients. Now it's up to your imagination to put together the right romantic and sensuous atmosphere and prepare your menu for your aphrodisiac feast.

CHAPTER VII
ROMANCE & SEDUCTION FALLING IN LOVE

Most people think of candlelight, music, flowers, a sunset or an exotic dinner when they think of romance and love. However, romance and seduction go much deeper because they involve the chemistry between two people—the inner feelings. Candlelight, music and perfume will enhance the romantic atmosphere, but they will never replace the true feelings and chemistry between people. This chapter will guide you through the romance and seduction elements that are necessary to get that someone special to react to you in the way you desire.

Cardinal Rule

> Seduction can be used to satisfy a person's deepest longings for fulfillment.

Before we can understand the full scope of romance and seduction and the role it plays in a relationship, we have to define the components that create the emotion of love.

Love has always been a topic that's been elusive for most people to grasp. One of the oldest concepts regarding what love is came from Plato, who believed love was a yearning to develop a togetherness. As people became civilized they created a sense of personal isolation and man had a deep need to fulfill a togetherness. Love provides man with the togetherness of bringing two people into one union. This need for togetherness has long been thought of as one of the defining characteristics of love. However, in the past 20 years, research has discovered key personality aspects that are directly involved with starting the flow of romantic feelings, or what we call love. Psychologists discovered that just three basic components of a person's identity are important. **They are gender, social persona and self ideal.**

These components are the deepest aspects of everyone's identity. For this reason, these three variables have the greatest impact on a person's feelings and why they fall in love. Love is something that develops from within the person's own psyche. In other words, the stimulation of these three areas is what gives birth to love. **Knowing how to stimulate these areas is what we describe as seduction.**

Love usually begins on the basis of the chemistry between two people and how they are going to respond to each other's personalities. During the courtship period, people will discover each other's characteristics and respond to the areas that are compatible with their self identity. As people become more involved and passionate, they experience within themselves fulfillment of their needs, and their true personalities or social self images begin to emerge. This will allow the relationship to gain strength and a sense of identity and eventually the people will feel complete and will fall in love with each other because in each other they see a reflection of both their inner desires and needs. The three key factors are:

1. Gender identity (masculine or feminine)
2. Social self image
3. Self ideal (characteristics of what a person truly is)

These three factors play a major role in whether a person will fall in love and with whom they will fall in love with. Unfortunately, most people are not aware of this and have no idea what to look for in another person. They are attracted by superficial appearances and use hit and miss techniques in trying to make the most important decision in their life, namely finding the right person for a long-term relationship. As society is proving today, lady luck does not usually stand by their side. Unfortunately, many go through life hopping from one relationship to another, continually searching, constantly recuperating from a seemingly endless series of emotional cuts and scrapes.

Self ideal is the feelings one has of worthiness. Most individuals have a desire to improve and achieve. When an individual feels content and self satisfied, subconsciously they will look for someone who supports, compliments and improves their self image. Because love is very deep and involves very deep emotions, and because all of us want to have a satisfying and rewarding relationship, we must pay attention to the affairs of the heart and those things that pull on our heart strings. Once you have an understanding of the components that make up love and once you have started into a relationship, you will be able to familiarize yourself with the aspects of personality in others and what is important for you to do in order to develop that relationship. You will be able to put together the information that we're outlining here in order to create the passion and feelings that you desire to create in your relationship.

Focusing on the Other Person's Needs

You must focus on the needs of your partner because your goal is to get your partner to fall in love with you. Through romance and seduction your purpose is to find the best ways to satisfy the desires and needs of the other. When a person is in love they experience a sense of completeness—a pleasant satisfaction. This feeling is what develops in response to the person that they are with. In other words, when you reinforce your partner's self image, you create a state of well-being. The lover creates a feeling of self esteem and satisfaction. The person's feeling of love many times encompasses their self worth, and you, in romancing and seduction, create that feeling of self worth and satisfaction. You validate the other person's value. Do not take lightly a person's need for approval. As our society has become more complex, everyone looks for approval from others. That is why belonging to organizations, groups, or social clubs gives a person a sense of worth. However, the greatest sense of worth comes from their lover. When somebody really feels loved, it causes the greatest impact on their self identity.

If you want to create joy in your partner, learn to respect their needs and their self identity and ego. How you feel about them has a very important effect on how they love you because it reflects directly on how they feel about themselves. Remember in the first section when we talked about the building steps in a relationship? Make sure not to criticize, give your lover enough space and have empathy for his or her feelings and beliefs. These building blocks are necessary in order to develop a deep, strong relationship. When a person falls in love, that person's sense of who they are and what they can do creates the depth and width of their love for their partner.

Even though people may feel they love someone because of the features or attributes that they have, it is really the feelings within their own mind that you have inspired in them, the qualities they desire and you're admiration for those qualities in them that has created the link between the two of you. Unless your lover feels valuable to you and to themselves, your love will not pass the test of time.

I have attempted to define, in a concise manner, the components that cause love, or the feeling of love in a person. The emotion of love is really a reflection of ourselves in others, and the links of our personality interwoven with another.

In order to develop a relationship with someone you desire, you need to apply the information that we discussed and how it will impact the other person.

Unfortunately, there are endless theories and books written about love. The purpose of this chapter is not to explore the entire world of love, but to give you a concise grasp of the key elements that compose the feeling of love with another person so that we can now explore the ways to use romance and seduction to fuel these components of love.

Cardinal Rule

Love and seduction deal with a person's self-identity and the 3 key components of love.
1. Gender identity (masculine or feminine)
2. Social persona (social self-image and role)
3. Ideal self (self-ideal—traditional—unconventional or dysfunctional)

Seduction

In essence, seduction of a person is being able to see and understand that person in the same way they see and feel about themselves in terms of their own self image. Once you've accomplished that, you reinforce that self image in the other person. That is what creates the element of love.

Love grows out of the combination of components that are the basic parts of each individual's self identity. There are three such elements. The first is the sense of gender. This component focuses on how the individual perceives their own masculinity or femininity, and how they act out their specific gender role. The second element is the sense of togetherness. That is the social self. The third is their feeling of their own self worth and potential. This is called the ideal self image, or ideal self. These are the deepest and strongest emotional factors of a person. When you play these components as a harp string, they create the sound called love.

A lot of people associate sex drive with love. As Freud describes it, the sex drive doesn't evaporate into thin air when it cannot be directly expressed. Instead, it will build into a sort of ground swell that comes out in the form of either sexual desires or romantic thoughts and feelings. However, what we are really describing is a person's gender identity and our need for sex without reason. It has put us in a position where we do not feel whole without an individual of the opposite sex. The acquisition of this other person or half creates and gives us the feeling of great pleasure that we call love. This point is supported by the reverse feeling of separateness. Being separated causes anxiety. This anxiety we call loneliness. When we overcome our loneliness and find the other half, we go from loneliness to togetherness to love.

We could discuss many ingredients or components that go into the recipe for love. However, the key ingredients are the ones we need to focus on. Although there are other ingredients that make up our self image, the key components of gender, social persona and self ideal are the predominant components that affect our feeling of love. These items affect us on such a basic level that the other components simply don't play as major of a role. This is the underlying reason why men and women do things in a relationship that can never be explained, or why two people in different circles are attracted to each other, and why throughout history people have done things in the name of love that could not be understood.

A seducer gives his loved one a feeling of self satisfaction and self worth. That is the reason love directly touches the most important personal aspects of our self identity. Love is not something that someone wears on their shirt sleeve. It is a distinct, internal emotion. It is a whole body experience. It is the experience a person feels when they combine the feelings of self satisfaction, encompassing the sexual, social and ideal aspects of their identity.

Once you comprehend these components and how they combine to give the feeling of love, you are able to direct your actions toward the one you wish to seduce in order to accomplish the desired results.

The illustration below will show how romance and seduction play in the ring of love.

♡ Love's Path ♡

Your Lover's hopes -needs-wishes -desires-goals -longings	You seduce using empathy to find the really crucial needs of your lover	You confirm and satisfy your lover's needs, hopes, longings	You create fulfillment and joy and the emotion of *LOVE*

When a person is falling in love they are experiencing an all encompassing feeling involving the three key components of the personality and those components are being fulfilled and satisfied. Therefore, when you are romancing or seducing a person you are working on their inward feelings in which the sexual, social and personal identity of what they believe their ideal is have been stimulated, excited and then gratified.

Seduction is when you use your familiarity of love's components to create the desired responses. You become the seducer. The seduced has a belief that their personal value and desires are about to be appreciated and fulfilled.

The illustration below shows in a progressive manner what happens during the process of seduction.

Discover Their Longings	The seducer understands,	Seduced reaches a
Will he stay with me forever	appreciates and then…	level of satisfaction
Does he enjoy being alone with me	confirms the women's sense, or identify and	and joy, result is a union of a man and
Does he appreciate me	longings, thus creating	woman
Does he think I look good	fulfillment and a sense	
Does he understand me	of worth and self-ideal	
Does he support my goals		
Does he feel we belong together		
Does he have the same values		
Does he feel I have worth		

I will try to explain in another way. Most people are thoroughly conditioned to act in a way that is in line with society's definition of gender roles. Each environment and culture create distinctive roles for each sex. As history has proven, people have the tendency to act out the roles society assigns to them. The Hite reports strongly affirms that many of the characteristics of our gender roles are defined by our environment and culture.

Once you realize this, you are prepared to understand that people are overly concerned about their bodies and their sexual identities. Very few people ever feel really secure. No matter what their experiences have been, people often feel unsure and compare themselves against standards of their gender or society. Therefore, men are always trying to secure and prove their masculinity and women are trying to prove and secure their appeal and femininity. Just look at any magazine and the ads within will substantiate this concept. As a result, everyone's sexual identity needs to be confirmed by a member of the opposite sex because we are disposed to a strong emotional reaction whenever we receive an approving response.

Whenever two people come together and are playing their sexual role and the other person appears a bit turned on, it supports, satisfies and gratifies the other person's gender identity. It is this support and gratification that we are each yearning for.

However, because of the different cultures, societies and environments that we have each experienced, how individuals obtain this gratification and affirmation is different. Everyone does not respond the same way to the same stimuli. For example, it is really our heart and our head that play a much greater role in stimulation than our lips and genital area. It is the process of that anticipation that many times will create great excitement or a romantic atmosphere. It is how we create this romantic atmosphere and seduce the other person that is important. There is a wide range of things that can be done to create a romantic atmosphere, but they will not always be received or appreciated by the other person in the same way, or create the acceptance and gratification. For some, the anticipation of a candlelight romantic dinner in an exotic place may cause feelings of desire. For others, the romantic trigger can be a picnic in a park, sharing a blanket at a concert, or relaxing on the deck of a yacht. The need and gratification for each is the same, it's just the vehicle or messenger that is different. That is where you, as a seducer, have to find out which vehicle to use to create the desired result. By working through the steps in developing a relationship that we have discussed, you should be able to have a feeling and direction of your lover's needs and wants. You should be able to anticipate what words, gestures or events will stimulate and gratify your lover the most.

Before we go on to discuss some of the techniques that you can use in seducing someone, I would like to point out that there is no firm rule or guarantee of certain results. In talking to many people over the years regarding different techniques that we have researched or experimented with, we find the responses are not always the same for a variety of reasons.

People react differently to different stimuli because there is a great deal of anxiety and uncertainty involved concerning love. Unfortunately in today's society, a lot of men and women have not had good role models to learn from. Often, their environments are poor. Because of the high divorce rate and proliferation of broken or dysfunctional homes, many have been raised with a distorted viewpoint of what relationships, self identity and gender identity are all about. In many circumstances it can cause the person to become unreceptive to the normal stimuli, or may produce great anxiety and insecurity.

In today's society it is sometimes very difficult to understand and perceive the social impulses and individual needs because there is such a strong tendency in our society to be impersonal to each other. The close community ties that we had two and three generations ago have now been disbanded through our mobile society and through the onslaught of our media. Each day, through television and other forms of mass media, we are confronted with outrageous happenings and facts that it makes many of us not only feel apprehensive, but insecure. As a result it creates another layer, or filter, of apprehension that we have to work our way through when we are trying to seduce someone. That is why we are seeing more and more people actively dating and having a number of encounters. Such individuals often fail to find the person that is really their soul mate, the person who can create the kind of fulfillment and gratification that they are looking for. Anyone who is in their late 20's or 30's is probably already experienced this at least once in their lifetime and understands that a very strong physical attraction can be the beginning of a short lived relationship. Therefore, we must be careful and very conscientious to become good listeners and discipline ourselves to follow through with the steps in developing a relationship in order to develop the type of loving relationship that we desire.

Because lovers not only relate to each other on the surface with sexual acts, but through the emotional bond, the reality of today's world is that although the physical act of sex has become more permissible, fewer and fewer people know how to develop the true emotional love bond. Although we all have these feelings and impulses for romance, love and relationships, many of us only work on the surface level with the sexual ingredients of love and not with the deeper emotional ingredients. Without these deeper emotional ingredients, the love is shallow and will not pass the test of time.

Therefore, what the information regarding romance and seduction really tells us is that because of the tremendous deep feelings love creates, one of the most important goals that we can accomplish when we are seducing a person is to create a warm rapport. The object is to relate to one another in such a personal way that each feels that they belong with each other, and that each compliments and supplements each other's self ideal and gender requirements.

The real act of seduction occurs when one induces love in another person through encouragement and reaffirmation of their values and self ideal. This is the seducer's ultimate goal. When you accomplish this in the eyes of your lover, you have obtained a status above all others. You have created a bond and link that places you in a special realm. Although you may look and act ordinary to everyone else, in your lover's mind you are exceptional. That is why sometimes the simplest of actions or gestures can be so meaningful to your partner.

Ways to Romance and Seduce

Although love has many facets, the three key components that define and develop the emotion of love are within your grasp. You are in a position, through romantic gestures and ways of seduction, to influence the person that you desire to fall in love with you. What you have to do at this point is to concentrate on the underlying motives of your partner and show your appreciation and fulfillment of these motives so that your partner will feel both appreciated and gratified and respond in the affectionate way that we label love. You have to first be able to show your approval of the other person's physical attractiveness, giving them both a feeling of security and appreciation. Then you must respond to them in a particular way to create the rapport that says you both should be together and that you agree and support with their social ideal. Then you must be able to reaffirm those things that will validate and confirm the ideal side of their identity.

Basically, seduction is the capability of conveying to the other person both the appreciation of their self ideal and the confirmation that you are pleased with the kind of person they are and the kind of companion they make. You demonstrate that you understand their characteristics and affirm that you appreciate the qualities and gifts they possess. In doing this, that person will be drawn to you because of the gratification that they feel and the satisfaction that you create in them. Thus, the bonds of love are created because of the pleasurable feelings that you have produced. To determine what techniques of romance will work for your particular seduction, you must take the time to listen carefully and find out the specific aspects of your partner's personality that you must appreciate and reaffirm. In order to do this you must go back to the steps that we discussed in developing a relationship. At this point, many of the steps that we have outlined that are important in developing a relationship will give you the key ingredients of where you can be most effective in seducing your partner in love. The steps in building a relationship will help you avoid the pitfall many people stumble into when they become mainly concerned about exterior qualities and their own self interests and desires. Remember, seducing a person is not about making your desires and likes the desires and likes of the other person, but of finding out what

Hilton Works
Primary Operations
A Responsible Care Area

"PRIMARY OPERATIONS UPDATE"

For: February 6, 2002

STELCO-PROUD PEOPLE CREATING VALUE

Hilton Works Quality Policy

" Hilton Works is committed to meeting our customers' requirements through continuous improvement of our processes, steel products and services. This will be accomplished by the involvement and dedication of all employees to ongoing Customer Satisfaction."

"Your Morning Smile"

If you'd like to have some company, just leave the house messy.

Health & Safety

B.O.F.
R.C.O.   Employee relates gradual onset of right shoulder pain from operating track switches.

social impulses they have and showing how you can appreciate and fully gratify them. This is when you really show your skill as a seducer and a great lover. You have then gone beyond the surface and have become totally involved with their internal emotions and needs.

The seducer becomes more impressed with the inner qualities of a person then those that are on the surface. It is through the appreciation and gratification of these inner qualities that the seducer creates a bond of love. As a seducer you must learn the art of a subtle compliment, understand what excites a person emotionally and be able to appreciate that fact so that you are able to have sensitivity and react in such a manner that you accommodate the person that you want to fall in love with. You must be able to strike the proper chords of their desires in such a manner that will give them both satisfaction and excitement. It may sound like a lot at first, but once you are into the rhythm of romance it will become easier and easier. The joys that you will experience are worth the effort,

Applying Seduction

What kind of reactions you receive from your partner will be largely governed by their memories and past experiences. The seducer must concentrate on supporting and reaffirming the positive, while downplaying the negative.

No emotion or reaction can be isolated from any given situation because a variety of experiences and identity factors come into spontaneous play. However, seduction can be used because we already are predisposed to certain romantic responses. For example, because of our gender identity and ideal self image, when a woman tells a man he looks very masculine and handsome, the man would be predisposed to react favorably because it involves his need to confirm his sense of worth and masculinity.

Cardinal Rule

> Affirmation of your lover's self-worth is the key tactic for evoking the emotion of love. However, do not over do it, or your words and actions will appear to be transparent or false.

The conditioning from our schools, family and media make all of us react in a predisposed way to certain statements or actions. Boys are taught to act macho and aggressive in the pursuit of sex. Girls are taught to act feminine and be the care givers at home. All these values are reinforced by our peers and media culture because all too often people are ridiculed when they do something different or wrong. For example, it would not masculine if a teenage boy cried because a girl did not call him when she said she would.

Understanding that people are in need of confirmation of their values and are predisposed to react in certain ways, we can now apply the different techniques of seduction to obtain the desired results.

Cardinal Rule

> A seducer confirms his or her lover's self-ideal by appreciating their values.

Everyone to some degree possesses this automatic emotional responsiveness. This process makes seduction possible. It is the conditioning of emotional responsiveness and a person's tremendous need to confirm their sense of self worth that enables you to seduce someone. When you appreciate one's values and worth and confirm those values and self worth and combine that with the three major components of love, you produce a feeling of not only self worth but satisfaction and joy in that person. This produces the emotion of love.

When you analyze the process we have just described, it begins to make sense why people will overlook many faults at times in both the individual and in the relationship because this underlying need for confirmation of their sense of self and identity is so commanding an emotion.

Although the romantic aspects of courtship are important in trying to create a nice environment, it is really how you affect that person that is all important. Although superficial qualities such as appearance or wealth may first attract a person, it is not the building block on which you can build a relationship. **A word of caution**—do not ever fall into the trap that by believing you can make someone else fall in love with you, that you will fall in love with them. Real love is never certain. When you are getting involved with someone you may find that their priorities and self worth conflict with yours and it is impossible for them to reciprocate your emotions. Therefore, realize this early so that you do not create a situation of a bittersweet romance. This is another reason why it is so important to follow the steps as we've discussed earlier in developing a relationship. Although the information we are giving you in this section will show you how to win someone's heart, you want to make sure that you are not setting you and the other person up for an emotional battle that will leave you both scarred.

Using the information that we've discussed in the 24 steps will enable you to help distinguish whether or not a potential lover has the capability of returning the love and confirmation of your self worth that you will need in order to have a relationship bond and grow.

Working through the 24 steps to developing a relationship will assist you in recognizing the components and the inner character of the person you are courting. This is necessary so that you will be in a position to confirm their sense of worth. Sometimes people simply don't know themselves as well as they believe and it is only through communication and interaction with the person in their life that they will be able to recognize when they are really expressing a significant personal aspect about themselves. In some cases, because of the personality and character traits, some people may consciously protect their ego or be in a defensive mode because of having some emotional scars. In such cases, you will have to deliberately be more attentive and sensitive while going through the 24 steps of a relationship to determine the true aspects of their identity.

Given enough time each of us will talk to a concerned listener and project their traits and their image of the type of person they believe they are. Once they have revealed enough, you will then be in a position to intentionally start the process of seduction by properly responding and showing your appreciation of their values and confirming their self identity, which in turn creates gratification, satisfaction, enjoyment and most importantly intimacy. A word of caution—if you are too superficial or too anxious, and do not discriminate between the superficial values and the true values of self worth, you will not obtain the desired results. The strategy of seduction will only succeed when you sincerely put forth the effort to affirm the unspoken but deepest desire of your lover. Using the 24 steps to develop a relationship will give you the opportunity and the insight to resolve the greatest needs and desires of the partner and enable you to complete the act of seduction by affirmation of their values and self worth.

One final note, love is very much like medicine. It is not a pure science that can be defined in black and white. There is a great deal of gray area. What we have attempted to do in a brief and concise manner is to show you the most direct path in seducing a person where you can create a feeling of love.

Another variable is that you may become so infatuated with the person that you are trying to seduce that you are seduced by them and your objectivity will not be clear. You may end up unknowingly making a lot of sacrifices or have the willingness to sacrifice your values to please them. However, in doing this it is very possible your needs will not be appreciated. Eventually your self worth and self identity will not be fulfilled and there will always be a wanting on your part.

The following section will give you a general idea of how to apply the knowledge that we have defined and discussed in this chapter.

You must nurture your lover's self ideal, but do it at a natural pace. If you try to rush the response you could turn the person off and have them withdraw. The growth of your lover's passion and emotion will begin when they recognize that you can appreciate their special value and worth.

This process will not happen every time you are together or as planned, however, with a succession of encounters the romantic bond will automatically build and will result in attracting your partner's heart and intention.

Cardinal Rule

> The whole process of seduction is based in part on what a person is experiencing and feeling in their lives at that time, so depending on a person's prior experiences and mood, a comfortable, safe, romantic, exciting or familiar atmosphere may influence the results.

If you are not currently interested or involved with someone, then start out with the idea of finding someone possessing the ideal traits you'd desire in a mate. Too often people leave their romantic involvement to pure chance. Many times circumstances work against the relationship, throwing up numerous obstacles. You do not wish to become involved in a bitter-sweet relationship because you'll end up always hoping that things will change for the better, and they never do. Too many people are attracted by outward appearances only and become emotionally involved with a person before they really find out the traits and qualities that they need or desire in a mate. That is why so many relationships are often doomed to frustration and anxiety. Do not allow yourself to fall into this pitfall. Do not be tempted by outward appearances only. Give yourself and your mate time to get to know each other.

Cardinal Rule

> The seducer should find someone who possesses the qualities that they desire and admire in a mate. Then the seducer can truly appreciate and affirm the other person's self worth and value. Your desire will further enable you to seduce the person by confirming their self ideal.

When you relate to someone that you already admire, this will increase your ability to seduce that person because the motivation is greater. Using a realistic approach to seduce someone that you already admire and appreciate makes your job easier. The obvious reason is that you are more likely to create the love and relationship that you desire and that will stand the test of time.

Although realistically you should have your preferences in order, it is important to understand that you will never find a mate that is completely perfect and meets all of your standards and expectations. Even the closest match will possess some characteristics that might irritate you. No matter how well suited you feel, you will have to compromise and adapt and work it out. That is why it is so necessary to go through the 24 step program in developing a relationship to make sure that you work out any problems or opinions before you make a long term commitment, or before you are too deeply in love and try to overlook the faults and characteristics that may turn out to be major obstacles in the future.

If you are patient and realistic and follow the 24 step program as well as the techniques that we have defined in this chapter on romance and seduction, you can be fairly confident about your seductive powers. Once you've found the person you desire and have attracted that person to you, you will be able to develop the emotion and passion that you are looking for in a relationship.

Cardinal Rule

> A lover gives the one who feels loved a valid reason to feel self-satisfied and fulfilled.

CHAPTER VIII

ON THE ROAD TO LOVE

You are now ready to go out and look for the potential love of your life. However, when starting out, make sure you take along self confidence and the right attitude. Self confidence and attitude can make the difference between success or frustration when you prospect for a new partner. Case studies illustrate that those who are overly apprehensive have a lot of emotional scars or misgivings and are more apt to communicate these apprehensions when they meet someone and are never given the opportunity to start a relationship. Also, people who have a negative, pessimistic attitude many times are predestined to fulfill their wishes and expectations of failure.

The first characteristic that other people are likely to pick up on is your attitude. By nature, people enjoy being around someone who is friendly, positive, relaxed and has reasonable expectations. This person is more suitable and you are then more likely to find and seduce that potential partner and lover.

However, as we discussed in the *Chemistry of Love*, there is always an element of chance and pure luck regarding the chemistry between two people. Do not be discouraged or upset if when you set out to find your partner the first person that you choose does not work out. Sometimes the initial chemistry just isn't right at the time for the two of you to become involved.

Life is an emotional journey, and when we start off our bags are filled with strong, uplifting emotions. We have trust, faith, love, hope, determination, pride and desire. These emotions can at times make us fly along the journey of life. However, as time goes on we hit obstacles and end up picking up new baggage to carry along. That baggage is very heavy and is filled with despair, loneliness, pain, frustration, anxiety, mistrust, and greed. Sometimes we come to a major turning point in our life and we have to go across a very high bridge. For some of us who have all that old baggage with us, it is very difficult to cross that bridge because we must drag that baggage along with us. Others are able to walk across the bridge while some are able to run because they are able to leave the old heavy baggage behind. You must be able to leave the old baggage behind, no matter how terrible you feel your experiences were in a previous relationship. If you insist on dragging that old baggage into a new relationship you will weigh down the whole affair. It will not have a fair opportunity to mature and develop into the relationship you really want and desire. You cannot bring mistrust, anger and hatred into a new relationship and expect it to develop into a warm, loving, satisfying and fulfilling relationship. No matter how difficult it may be, you must conscientiously make the effort to free your mind from its apprehensions. Discard the old heavy, negative baggage and just retain the good, positive baggage that we start off with.

Cardinal Rule

> A strong, loving relationship can make everything a little more bearable.

Realistically, you shouldn't make a snap judgement about people and their characteristics or their outward appearance when you first meet them. That is why going through the 24 steps to a relationship are so important. It gives you both the time and space to make a solid contact with a person and get their true reactions to your characteristics and needs. This is so very important if you want to avoid the situation that is commonly heard in divorce counseling. "He/she was an entirely different person after we got married. I never really knew him/her."

Personal rejection is a difficult thing for everyone. However, many times because a person doesn't accept your first invitation, it should not be taken as a personal rejection. Some people who are very shy will need a little time and space. Give them an opportunity to know the real you. You will see in many situations they will warm up and become comfortable. As we discussed in the prior chapter, a good seducer is also a good listener. You must be able to perceive the person's needs and longings so that you can appreciate and confirm them. Remember, someone may be a little shy, nervous or just having a bad hair day. Give them a second, or even a third opportunity. In between, try to let them know or see a little more of you. Find out the type of things they like to do so that your next encounter can be on familiar ground.

One final note, perhaps the other person is not ready to have love and a relationship enter into their life. Perhaps the other person has too much heavy baggage and cannot let it go. Do not become desperate and try to overcome all the obstacles in their life. There's nothing to be done until that person is ready to remove the obstacles themselves or make a change in their life. Experience has taught us that in the vast majority of cases you cannot change a person or remove their obstacles for them. You are better off keeping your self confidence. There are many single people out there who are looking for happiness and love as much as you are. You will be more prone for success if you look for a person who is at the same readiness level that you are for love.

Cardinal Rule

> Attempt to meet and socialize with people in places that you like and that make you feel good and comfortable. Chances are the person you meet there will feel the same as you. Visit places that have the atmosphere and the type of people and that put you in a good mood.

By conscientiously choosing the right atmosphere, your mood will remain positive and you can focus your attentions on the people you are meeting because you will feel comfortable and secure.

Cardinal Rule

> When people experience the same reaction to something together they have a tendency to feel a closeness because in reality they are sharing a common emotion. Many times this will give each of them a sense of belonging and draw them closer together. When the seducer can create this emotion there will be instant gratification and the seduced will want this type of closeness to continue.

Another advantage of frequenting places where you enjoy the atmosphere and the people is that you are more likely to continue feeling enthusiastic and optimistic about meeting the right person because chance does come into play. You have to be patient. It may not be the first, second, third, or fourth day when you meet the right person. However, having the right attitude and being in the right atmosphere will keep your poise and mood positive and you will be prepared when that right someone comes along. Furthermore, take comfort in the fact that the vast majority of men and women have to deal with the same situation and lifestyles that you do today and most of them have the same yearnings and attitudes as you do. They are hoping and waiting for real love to come into their life.

The final step is also the first step, and that is overcoming your nervousness and anxiety in regards to meeting someone and starting the process of seduction. Whether you start with a smile, a glance of the eyes, or an overt approach, you must take that first step. If someone catches your eye and hasn't noticed your presence, maneuver yourself in a place to at least give that first glance, smile or eye contact. If it is received with a like smile or eye contact, then follow up. It often doesn't matter what the first remark is, but if you can't think of anything to say, a friendly "hi," can always start a conversation. Once the conversation is started the other person will usually offer their opinion on something, and that is your signal to pick up on the topic and follow through. Once you make the initial connection you can change the topic and the conversation will move along. During that first contact, people must make a decision if they are going to see you again or not, and usually they have very little to go on. So during this first contact, you need to make them feel that you are on the same emotional and intellectual wavelength. This is the most you can hope for in that first meeting. They will also have to make a decision to take it on face value. This has to do with what we refer to as sexual chemistry and appearance. This may not always be the best basis to make a judgement, however, that is what people usually do. The best you can hope for during the first meeting is being able to possibly compliment someone's gender identity. This can usually create a bond and an interest to see someone in the future because affirming their gender identity has produced a favorable impression upon them and confirms that you appreciate them for themselves.

Cardinal Rule

One of the deepest romantic longings a person can have is to meet another person who feels the same way about things as they feel, and to be able to share a happening, event or attitude together. This serves to bring the people closer together as if they were one sharing the same experience.

During the first meeting you will have a tendency to move on to different issues, sometimes issues generating passion. A word of caution—do not move too quickly into these matters because the other person may be too unsettled or nervous to give serious thought or concentration to these matters, or it may make them feel uncomfortable. Try to keep the conversation casual and look for areas where you can reinforce each other's gender identity.

Most of the time the relationship on its own will develop and eventually you will get to the point where you're going to ask for that first date. The first date, at best, is kind of an audition for each other. It can cause a lot of pressure sometimes for people to put on appearances and formalities. However, try to make your first date in a setting that will induce relaxation and communication for both of you. Most people think that a romance should be fast, exciting and adventurous. Many people want to be swept off of their feet by a new partner. They may try to create a rapid pace. However, this can create two problems. First, it may be offensive and make the other person nervous. Secondly, as we have discussed in the fundamental components of a relationship, moving too fast can many times get people too physically involved too soon. This is one of the main reasons why new relationships fail to get off the ground. Incompatibilities and problems come up very quickly in the relationship before you have had an opportunity to build a strong basis and a good line of communication and trust, which is necessary in order to resolve or mediate differences or problems.

It is during this first date that you as a seducer should be prepared to start developing the process that we have discussed in this and the prior chapter regarding romance and seduction. You will begin to set both the stage and the tone for the relationship. Be prepared because it may move along very quickly. Emotion is not something that you are always able to control or channel. It is important for you to keep the other person's attention and interest so you can apply the techniques that you have studied regarding seduction and romance. It is not good enough to think about something, you must act upon it. You must be able to verbalize your feelings and your intentions. Do not doubt yourself. If you do, your prophesy of failure will come true.

If you apply the things you learned in the components of a relationship, the 24 steps, and apply the basic fundamentals that we have outlined in romance and seduction, you will be well on your way to creating the emotional responses and feelings that you so desire in a relationship. Once you start the emotion going you will also be the recipient of love. This is the beauty of love. It is a self-fulfilling passion that nurtures itself if given the opportunity and will create mutual feelings of appreciation, satisfaction and happiness.

Cardinal Rule

> Since the process of love creates many emotional responses, many times the seducer can become the seduced in a relationship because things will evolve at a very rapid pace and the passion between the people involved can cause such a stimulus to their gender identities and self worth that roles can easily be changed.

Chemistry and timing are important factors in the development of love. Sometimes a woman and man who are attracted to each other seem to have many compatible interests and attitudes, however, they are unable to develop an intimate emotional relationship. The usual reason that they cannot develop a closer relationship is because either one or the other or both has a great deal of anxiety and is reluctant to be honest and intimate with the other person for fear of being disappointed, criticized or ridiculed. Thus, they are unable to move on to the next level of emotional commitment. You have to realize that in some situations you may not be able to do or say anything that will change this. However, working carefully through the 24 components that we discussed may create the bridge that is necessary for the relationship to continue.

Cardinal Rule

> The master key to unlocking the deepest emotions is based upon the seducer's ability to discover the seduced's unconscious anticipation of what a romance and their ideal mate should be, and then to accept and confirm those feelings in the seduced. This can usually produce a torrent of emotion for the seducer.

Chapter IX

The Power of Touching

Touching someone is a powerful form of communication. There are all forms of compassionate touching. The touch of the right person can start the adrenaline running wild and rushing through you making you feel breathless. You must master the techniques of the touch and caress. Touching will give a whole new dimension to your sexual relationship. This is especially important for people to develop to keep youth and passion in a marriage because many times over a period of time sex in a marriage will become predictable, almost mechanical, and frustration and boredom can set in and leave the desire for sex almost nonexistent. That is why this section is devoted to the power of the touch.

Cardinal Rule

> **Women have expressed that the need and desire to be held, touched and caressed is greater at times than the desire for intercourse.**

You must develop the techniques of foreplay. Good sex can start while your clothes are still on. Developing the sensuous mood can make the pleasure of a sexual relationship go on for hours, even days before having sexual intercourse. The feeling and mood that one develops is the sweetest of all sexual satisfaction. It puts one in a state of euphoria and tranquility. The tempo can build to a prelude that will make the adrenaline rush wild where your partner will go mad with desire for all the passions of the deepest pleasures of sex.

Touch is the most fundamental of our senses and the parent of all our other senses. In fact, touching and being touched is so powerful that people who do not come into contact with others often have feelings of depression. There is a slogan that one hug a day will keep you warm and comfortable. The power of touch does not diminish as we grow older. In fact, it is probably the most important element because touching is essential to our emotional and sexual lives and has a tremendous impact on our life and behavior.

Touching is a stimulator. All parts of the body are sensitive from the tips of your toes to the top of your head. When you touch someone you are sending a message. A touch can be reassuring, calming or sexually stimulating. Caressing and touching are important to our well-being and are key ingredients in a sexual relationship. The steps we have discussed to emotionally prepare one for a sexual relationship are necessary so that we can train ourselves emotionally to use the powerful sensitivity of touch in a sexual relationship.

Touching and the power of touching is so important that there have been numerous books written about the medicinal benefits of physical contact. Anyone from newborn infants to the elderly can reap the benefits of a touch or caress. There have been articles in the newspapers about therapeutic touching. The entire body is covered with skin and there are millions of tiny nerve endings that are touch receptive. All kinds of extraordinary reactions are set in motion when you touch or stroke the skin. Our senses, especially the sense of touch, are perhaps more important that our mental capacities at times because away a person caresses or touches someone is a greater communicator and can do more to convey a person's feelings than all the words that one can put together. A touch can bring feelings of release, love, pride, bravery and sensuousness more quickly than anything that we can communicate in any other way to another person. A mother's kiss on a sore can take away the pain instantly. A pat on the head can give pride and determination to a child. A hug or holding one's hand can bring release during a time of aggravation and anxiety. The laying on of hands has been a source of healing throughout the centuries. As we grow older we need more and more caressing and touching. Because so many in our society associate touching with sex play and intercourse, we refrain from using it. We miss out on the tremendous rewards of physical contact. Remember, a sensual touch can be like a sensual dream.

Cardinal Rule

> Through touch you can communicate understanding, compassion and love.

Sensuous touching should not be just part of the foreplay. It should become an involved intricate part of the whole sexual relationship. Touching can arouse places you never knew were sensitive. A sensual touch is one that creates feelings and gratifies the senses. It is sensuous, it is common, and it causes reaction. Touching both gives and receives. The giver can receive as much sexual satisfaction as the receiver. One leads to the other. Touching allows you to explore each other's bodies. The sensitive and sensuous lover can evoke a feeling of euphoria with their fingers. Once you are both calm and enjoying the sensitivity of touch, you can then create sexual excitement using different parts of your body along with your hands and fingers to give a rush of adrenaline to your partner and touch the hot spots or G spots of the body and create a burning and steamier desire than you have ever imagined possible. Creating a sensuous, exciting touch is an art form. It is a wonderful process and is not just a prelude to intercourse, because touching can so stimulate the body that people can experience sexual ecstasy and orgasms without even having intercourse. Touching and the sensation it creates is in and of itself a pleasure.

Touching is so powerful that it can linger in our bodies even when it is not actually happening. It can cause the body chemistry to react with such a rush that you can feel a rush of adrenaline and flutters in your stomach or in your groin. The sensation and feeling of being touched stays with you long after the experience.

The human body reacts physically to touching. Because of the sensuous feelings that are being transmitted through the touch, the skin can react around the sexual parts of the body. The nipples can take on a telltale color, warmth and firmness.

We must condition and prepare ourselves to be receptive to the touch. The steps and elements we discussed about emotionally preparing a person to enter into a sexual relationship are important to develop. No matter how much physical pleasure the touch may bring to an individual, if we are not emotionally ready to receive the caress of another, then we will not be able to fully react to the touch and sensitivity of our partner. We must be both emotionally and physically ready to seek out the tenderness and intensity of the physical pleasure of touching. If touching does not come from a partner who is emotionally ready and filled with love, it simply does not work as well. Once you're both on the same level and you have that intimacy connection, then the possibilities of stimulation and response are infinite, and the compassion that touching can bring to your sexual relationship is the most wondrous bonding that any will ever experience.

The need to be held, touched, and caressed, can be so great that some people hunger for it more than sexual intercourse.

Cardinal Rule

Never confuse the need for affection (hugging and touching) with sexual desire, otherwise you may never be satisfied.

Too many people associate kissing with touching in a sexual relationship. However, kissing is perhaps to some less stimulating and rewarding than the oral and manual stimulation of the genital areas. For many women, the touching, caressing and kissing of the breasts is a sexual arousal. When two people have developed a proper intimacy, they can each experience the pleasure of touching. People can learn to explore each other, not being concerned with just the erogenous zones of the body. As two lovers develop a feeling of sensitivity and intimacy and confide in each other about what stimulates them, they can learn to excite all parts of the body. True lovers can learn that by caressing or stroking the forehead, the ear, the chin, the inside thigh, the breasts, the chest, or the legs of their lover, they can create a delightful sensation and with practice can even cause a sexual frenzy. You must take the time to experiment. You must be honest with your partner and help them to learn what pleases you and what causes you the greatest pleasure. There is as much excitement for the person who is touching as for the person being touched and caressed. There is no one sure method that will excite everyone in the same way. However, as we will discuss, there are certain zones that create pleasure.

In order to implement the proper touching techniques, you must be familiar with the different parts of the body. Think of every part of the body, each inch of skin, as a sensual terrain for your fingers to explore.

In many parts of the world there are traditional beliefs or religious beliefs, even in today's society, that lovers and partners should not view each other naked or that they should refrain from touching or caressing certain parts of the body, whether in public or in private. This is very sad because in different parts of the world people who follow tradition are not even aware of the tremendous sensuality that touching has and of the many mental, emotional and physical benefits that touching and caressing creates. Touching, caressing and holding not only creates excitement and pleasure (especially when one is in the specific erogenous zones), but it satisfies a basic human need. Many people in society feel depressed at times or even fatigued when they really desire to be held, touched, or caressed. There are numerous research programs that have established the clear need and health benefits, both mental and physical, from being held and touched. In fact, in some studies, it has shown that the life force in a person can be renewed and regenerated by the love and the touching of another person at the right time. It is true that many people do not even realize that the hunger they have at times for lovemaking is really the desire to be touched and to be held, and sexual intercourse is only the by-product.

In today's society, because of media exploitation, many of us have been given the false impression of what true sex in a sexual relationship is and what we should obtain from that relationship. Although almost all advertising is predominantly sexually oriented, the attitudes that are presented are superficial. As discussed in the development steps of a sexual relationship, many emotional, mental, moral and physical things come into play in order to obtain a truly rewarding sexual relationship. The key in developing a physically rewarding sexual relationship is in the care taken in developing the body energy by caressing and touching. We all have strong and loving feelings and from the sensitive inside of our ears to the zones of skin between our toes and on our bottom of our feet, we are alive with nerve endings and receptacles receiving messages of pleasure and satisfaction. The older we get, the more important this becomes. Some women develop strong needs to be held and to be caressed and hugged as they mature. They can receive tremendous gratification along with emotional rewards by being touched and caressed and held by their lover.

Learning to caress and touch your partner may be fundamental in having them relax and relieve the tension and anxieties that are in the body so that they can enjoy their sexual relationship and receive more benefits from it. We will explore in detail the important role that anxiety plays in the sexual relationship. However, here it is sufficient to say that in order to really enjoy themselves they must be relaxed and at ease and receptive. A major benefit in foreplay is to learn to caress and touch in a such a way as to first relieve the tension, then replace the tension with a sensitivity of delight, and finally, excitement and anticipation. Sexual relationships should be rewarding and fulfilling for both partners. Keep in mind, it will pay big dividends in the long run to learn to bring both partners to the same level of enjoyment, thus obtaining a true level of intimacy in the relationship.

Learning to touch and caress someone in the proper way is so important because in many cases it can make one lightheaded, reach a level of euphoria, or even bring about sexual orgasms. Lying next to your lover and being caressed and held is as delightful for some as the young baby being held by its mother and being gently rocked to sleep.

In order to master the art of knowing how to pleasure yourself and your partner, you need to learn where to rub, stroke, apply pressure, caress, or touch. You need to not only know the different points of the body, you also need to understand how the zones of the body work. By now you should realize that the largest sex organ in the body is the skin. That is why it is so important to master the power of the touch in order to create the pleasures and responses that you desire.

The information that were going to cover or explore together now will enhance both the pleasure and excitement you receive in a sexual relationship, and it should also relieve the anxiety that confronts many people about sexual relationships. In our society today, a lot of importance is placed upon an individual in a sexual relationship. Men are under great stress because they feel that their masculinity is at stake and they need to prove their potency by their sexual performance. This not only causes a great deal of anxiety and panic in men, but as discussed in book two of the trilogy, it can become a major barrier in having a rewarding and pleasurable sexual relationship. Women are under no less pressure to perform sexually, and they are subjected to additional expectations. Many women feel pressured to forever look young, good looking, and sexually attractive. Sometimes it causes a great deal of anxiety and problems in a woman because she feels she is not desirable, that she has no self esteem and social value. Of course, the advertising media reinforces these standards and notions at every turn. The advertising media does not take into consideration all the steps that we've discussed in a sexual relationship, along with the character, intelligence, warmth, personality, social skills, compatibility and all the other things that go along with a sexual relationship.

A sexual relationship is an all encompassing activity. It involves the mind, emotions, and the entire physical body. Most people that think of the physical aspect of sex think of the sex organs. However, a sexual relationship and sexual activity involves the entire nervous system, hormones, adrenaline, and millions of nerve endings. All of this comes together in a sexual relationship. It's a response cycle. During the time of sexual touching and caressing, your entire system will become aroused and experience new sensations and feelings that are not normally felt at any other time. Usually this will take the form of a climax with an orgasmic sensation. Then there's a time of relaxation, rest, peace, contentment and a feeling of fulfillment. The cycle of response is the same regardless of age, sex, size or belief.

When all the emotional aspects of a sexual relationship are in place, then the physical aspects take over, especially the sensation of touch, which involves all of the body. The activation of the sex hormones plays a very important role in the responsiveness in each of the partners. The chemical steroids are produced in the adrenaline glands of both men and women, as well as in the ovaries of the woman and in the testes of the man. The hormones are released directly into the blood stream and are carried to the different organs of the body affecting both the functioning and appearance of these organs. The active female hormone, estrogen, will produce a profound affect on the development and functioning of the female sex organs. The male hormone, androgen, will influence the changes and desires in both men and women, as well as some of the sexual development in men. The pituitary gland is the regulator that adjusts and influences the hormone levels. There are thousands of things that are simultaneously going on in the body at the time of sexual arousal. Even today, medical science cannot clearly define and understand all the things that happen to the body during a sexual encounter. However, it is important in order to comprehend all the facets of touching and what pleasure or arousal can be brought about, that you have a basic understanding of some of the sexual and reproductive organs of both men and women.

Chapter X

Kissing is Love's Messenger

When two lips touch, it is the first taste of what is to come. It is the first thing to turn you on and to light your fire. It starts the romance and passion. A great kiss communicates one's desire and love to another.

Passionate kissing is the essence of romance and the beginning, middle and end of a good love encounter. How unfortunate that men and women leave themselves so vulnerable by being too shy, filled with anxiety, or the belief that passionate kissing is not proper. Thus they spoil the mood of a romantic encounter by disappointing themselves and their lover by poor kissing or lack of kissing. What a quick turn-off. No mater how attractive and sexy their lover may look, that first impression will last. Kissing dissatisfaction will decrease the level of passion and enjoyment. Poor kissing can spoil both the mood and desire, and over time decrease the intensity of lovemaking. When kisses lose their passion, it is a disappointment to both partners and the lovers may lose interest and desire in their relationship.

From our group discussions and numerous interviews, we have learned that kissing sends very clear messages. It is the messenger of love, especially for women. Passion, love, romance and care are all conveyed in a kiss. Sometimes a kiss can tell more about the relationship then any amount of words. Many times women can tell if the care and passion is slipping away and if the relationship is going off course by the way they are kissed.

Cardinal Rule

> Poor kissing is a real mood killer. Although there could be a torrent of passion beneath the surface, poor kissing sends the wrong message.

Good kissing should start your adrenaline going, fan the flames of desire and instill that tingly feeling of anticipation. Looks are very sensuous and can convey a lot of signals. Even the slightest gesture with the mouth can excite someone. Just the sight of a woman playing with her lips or tongue can drive many men wild with excitement.

When a man winks at a woman and blows her a kiss, it can cause more than a blush. The thoughts that this action generates can bring a rush of passion and desire. Never underestimate the power of lips and kissing in a relationship.

Cardinal Rule

> If your partner's kissing isn't as hot and passionate as you desire, communicate your feelings to them in a caring way and suggest to your lover how they could change their particular style of kissing.

Good kissing will create an inexplicable synergy between your lover that once experienced will always remain. Therefore, you should show your lover how much you enjoy kissing and show your lover how you most like to be kissed. When they do it the way you like it, praise him or her.

Both men and women's egos enjoy the feeling that they are exciting and pleasing their lover. It is a real ego buster when someone kisses like a bird pecking at a seed because it communicates to your partner a lack of passion and interest.

Passion and good kissing have many rewards. It not only shows that you appreciate your partner, as discussed in Romance and Seduction, it will reaffirm their self worth and gender identity in addition to the physical excitement and pleasure it causes. The impression it creates on the ego is long lasting after the physical act has ended.

Cardinal Rule

> Even a subtle kiss between lovers is a messenger of romance. When you kiss your lover when it is least expected, even if it is a light kiss on the forehead, back of the neck, or cheek, the love message is sent and is very clear and well received.

The lips are one of the most sensual instruments used in foreplay. As we've discussed in the prior chapter, your entire body is made up of sensuous skin. It is an enjoyment to both parties to explore all the areas and little crevices of their lover's body with their lips and tongue. In some people, this will cause tingling, enjoyment, excitement and anticipation. It can even drive some into a wild, passionate state of euphoria. This type of kissing is fun to both give and receive and can be done almost anywhere and any time. A tender kiss can be given on the back of a hand while you're seated at a table with your loved one. The right type of kiss at the right place can send a very clear message.

Communicate to your partner the pleasure of sensual kissing and learn what pleases each other. Is it the light kiss on the cheek? The tender kissing and fluttering on a nipple? Or is it a seductive type of kissing where one would suck on one's finger and kiss the inside palm of the hand? Or is it a full embodiment of French kissing where you press your lips firmly together while caressing each other tongues? Whatever form is most enjoyable for you, you must communicate that to your partner so you can keep the enjoyment, pleasure and anticipation in your relationship.

A number of interviews and surveys have revealed that a relationship begins to sour when there's a lack of passion and desire in the kiss. Many times women stated that they noted a distinct change in the kiss and did not mention it to their mates, only to find out later that both partners had become disenchanted and lost interest and it was then too late to re-flame the fire because the fire had gone out of the relationship.

Cardinal Rule

> **How you kiss shows your true feelings and intentions.**

People from all generations and backgrounds have shared one common interest about kissing. One of the important things that can be seen about a relationship is the affection shown through kissing.

When you kiss, your lips should be firm yet gentle enough so that the inside of the lips touch each other. Add a little tongue intermittently, gently at first until you achieve a rhythm and motion that is pleasing to both partners. Do not be too abrupt or harsh because this may cause some discomfort. At first go slowly, but do not keep your lips tight because this will be associated with a lack of passion. Usually the kissing will take up its own rhythm and lead into foreplay. The kiss should be soft, yet firm and should be tingling and exciting for both parties. Remember, kissing is the messenger of love.

Cardinal Rule

> The last kiss is the kiss that should never, ever be overlooked. This is the kiss that happens after a passionate night of lovemaking. Before you leave or retire, give your lover a hug and a passionate kiss. This one last kiss sends a real message that you truly care.

Kisses are sensual communications. Be generous with your kissing, not only in your lovemaking, but when you are saying goodbye, or even while working together at home, or when out together with the family. To show you how lasting the impression can be, one lady who had been married for over 60 years said that what she missed the most after her husband had passed away was his good morning kiss each morning before breakfast. I can not say anything more meaningful than that.

Kissing Tips

- Communicate to your partner how you like to be kissed.
- Show your partner how you like to be kissed so they know exactly how it feels and how you want it.
- If your partner kisses you in a pleasurable way, let them know that is the style and type of kiss you enjoy.
- Usually closed lips, tight lips, convey a kiss without passion or feeling.
- Find the hot spots on your partner's body that they enjoy having kissed. Some hot spots are nipples, toes, fingers, belly buttons, earlobes, the back of the neck, the back of the knees, certain back areas, palms of the hand, cheeks and forehead.
- Engage in playful kissing and tickling. Certain sensitive parts of the body are easily ticked and excited with your tongue and lips.

Cardinal Rule

French kissing is thought by many as the most passionate type of kissing. You develop a French kiss after pressing your lips gently together. Both kiss and suck each other's tongue. The key to good French kissing is to be able to develop some sort of rhythm. Move your tongue around and alternate sucking on each other's tongue. This type of kissing can become very passionate and can go on for long periods of time.

Sex and Our Anatomy

The reason that the following sections were written was to remove the veil of secrecy that for so long has inhibited so many people when dealing with a sexual relationship.

Everyone feels awkward about sexual relationships and their own sexuality and although we can all stumble into sexual intercourse, the studies and interviews reveal that many people *never* have a really fulfilling, satisfying, pleasurable sexual relationship.

Cardinal Rule

> Always develop a good relationship first. Sex should be a secondary matter. Always be intimate and honest.

Many people feel awkward and unsure about exactly how to have great sex and a rewarding relationship. Because of our ego and pride we are afraid to admit that they want to know more.

Most people's self-respect keeps them from looking for advice in the wrong places, which is good because they would only get the wrong information and there is already too much of that available.

The following sections were developed to help you build your knowledge, talent and skills along with your confidence to become a *great lover* and to capture the wonderful feeling of fulfillment and satisfaction in your relationship.

The veil of secrecy or the taboo about discussing sex in our schools and in our churches has lead to tremendous uncertainty in many people's minds regarding the sexual organs of the body. As a result, when you watch movies or television, see the billboards or read the numerous magazines, the media has been able to distort what sexuality is and how the perceived perfect body should look. However, let me assure everyone that this is not a true picture.

Each man has grown up with a natural curiosity about the length of his penis, nervous and afraid that he won't measure up. However, penises come in all sizes. The average erect penis is approximately six inches long. However, no matter how long or short the penis is, it does not matter in giving sexual pleasure. As far as sensitivity, they are equally sensitive to touch and excitement, and as far as the female response, only two to three inches of an erected penis is necessary. In arousing the female and satisfying her during the act of intercourse, only the first two inches or so of the vagina are sensitive. The average female vagina is about five inches long. The back portion is not sensitive at all and as we will discuss later in this text, the crucial pleasure spot for the female is the clitoris.

As much as our society obsesses about penis length, that's nothing in comparison to the amount of attention it lavishes on women's breasts. The media places tremendous importance upon women's breasts, as can be seen in advertising and in entertainment. However, breasts come in all sizes and shapes. Some may be firm and perky, while other's are soft and droopy. However, they all respond to stimulation and are equally sensitive to touch, excitement and arousal. A woman's breast size and shape will be continually evolving and changing during her life cycle. Women are constantly concerned about the shape and development of their breasts. Unfortunately, this can sometimes become a phobia or an emotional block with a woman feeling that if she does not have a certain size and shape of breast, that she will be unattractive and not as sexually pleasing. However, the sexual enjoyment and pleasure that a woman receives and the sensitivity that she feels is the same regardless of the size and shape of her breasts.

There is no medical research or proof to substantiate that increasing the size of a man's penis or the size of a woman's breasts will increase sexual responsiveness or pleasure. However, there are thousands of products that are promoted that give false hope or expectations to men and women by making unsubstantiated claims regarding benefits to either the penis or the breasts.

As long as all the proper elements are in place for a good sexual relationship, you can obtain as much satisfaction, gratification and pleasure as anyone. It is a false assumption that larger physical attributes lead to greater sexual pleasure. Each individual has the capability of reaching a rewarding and pleasurable sexual relationship regardless of the size of their physical characteristics.

Words alone cannot express the feeling of ecstasy and fulfillment that you will experience when you gain the self confidence and power to have a sexual relationship that you could only dream of before.

Cardinal Rule

Sex is the easiest thing we do; when we do it with the right partner. We should feel good and fulfilled. If you have any doubts or feel bad about it, then *don't* do it because if you make a bad decision with the wrong partner you could have a lifetime of regret.

Please have a medical exam and consult with a physician if you have any condition which precludes strenuous, sexually exciting activity.

Some of the explicit sexual techniques may be unfamiliar to you and may take practice to do proficiently. Please do so at your own risk.

Chapter XI

The Male Sexual Anatomy

Understanding how your sex organs function will help you become more responsive and understanding regarding the proper methods and pleasures that you can use during a sexual relationship. The male and female sex organs (genitals) are in a constant state of development and change from the time of birth until our death. The sex organs are also the reproductive organs of the body. When a man and woman have sexual intercourse and the man has an orgasm, sperm comes through his penis into the woman's vagina. If the sperm comes in contact with an egg in the uterus, then the woman can conceive and become pregnant (sperm can leak out of the penis and into the vagina without a man having an orgasm). The reproductive systems of both the male and female are very simple in design, yet very complex in how they function. It is the same reproductive system that creates the pleasure and gratification of a sexual relationship.

The male's genitals are the penis and the scrotum. The testicles, two separate oval shaped eggs that produce sperm, are located inside the scrotum. The male produces sperm in their testicles. When a male becomes aroused and sexually excited, the penis will become erect and very hard. When a man obtains an ejaculation or climax, it is called an orgasm.

The cone-shaped part of the penis, the glans, is very sensitive, as well as the back side of the shaft of the penis.

THE MALE ANATOMY:

Penis:	This organ is outside the male body. It is the organ that a man urinates with. It is also the sexual organ that during intercourse penetrates the females vagina. The end of the penis is usually cone-shaped and is referred to as the glans.
Testicles:	These are two separate oval-shaped eggs (balls) that produce sperm.
Scrotum:	The container or pouch of skin that holds the testicles and allows the sperm to be produced.
Vas Deferens:	This tube-like part enables the sperm to move from the epididymis and through the urethra to the ampulla.
Ampulla:	The enlarged end of the vas deferens. The ampulla is the staging area where the semen is made up from different body fluids along with the sperm.
Prostate :	The prostate is a gland that surrounds the neck of the bladder and the urethra. The function of the prostate gland is to produce a thin milky fluid that also mixes with sperm to help protect them during their travels.
Seminal Vesicle:	A mucus-like fluid is produced by this bag-like structure. This fluid then mixes with sperm and helps keep the sperm healthy.
Cowper's Glands:	Consists of two small round glands below the prostate gland. The purpose of these glands is to produce a mucous-like fluid that lubricates the end of the penis

before intercourse and to help the transport and protection of the sperm.

Urethra: The urethra extends from the bladder to the opening at the tip of the penis. This tube is what carries the urine or semen to the outside of the body.

Urinary Opening: Refers to the end of the penis and the slit or opening that urine and semen come out of.

Sperm: A sperm (spermatozoa) is a tiny egg that looks like a tadpole. It is this cell that joins with the female's egg to create a baby.

Semen: During sexual intercourse, a fluid is ejected from the urinary opening. The semen fluid is made up of seminal vaginal fluid, prostate gland fluid, a small amount of Cowper's Gland fluid, and sperm. During intercourse, it is the job of the semen to work it's way into a woman's uterus and to come in contact with the woman's egg.

Erection: The process where the penis changes from flaccid (soft) to erect (hard). This occurs when the man is aroused. The penis engorges itself with blood and become hard and erect.

Ejaculation: The process when semen comes out of the urinary opening of the penis.

Foreskin: Refers to the area of loose skin around the glans penis and the upper shaft of the penis. If a male is not circumcised, foreskin will refer to the cover of skin over the glans penis.

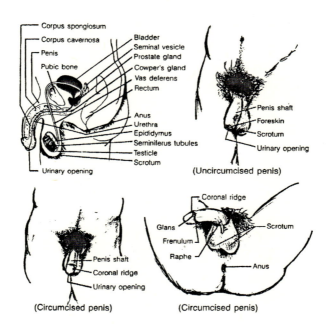

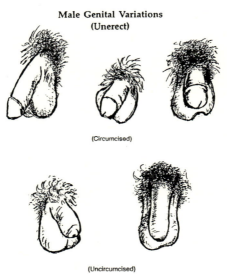

Male Reproductive System

The function of the penis is thought to be understood by most. However, "there is no organ about which more misinformation has been perpetuated," William Master, M.D., and Virginia Johnson of the Masters and Johnson Institute in Virginia once observed. "That amazing item of flesh has been venerated in cults, reviled and misrepresented in folk legends and mutilated, decorated, hidden, exposed, adorned and feared throughout the centuries. It is the item that is on every young man's mind as he grows up. It is the item that gives a great deal of frustration and anxiety because people are not sure how it should look, how it should perform, how they should treat it and how to properly use it."

Cardinal Rule

> Young men are caught up in the false big penis mythology and are always worried about how they measure up to others. However, the truth is that there is no correlation between penis size and sexual pleasure.

In truth, the reproductive cycle for the male is very simple. The male has two testicles. They are shaped like small eggs and held in the scrotum, a pouch of skin outside of the body. The purpose of the testicles is to produce the male eggs or cells which are called sperm. During intercourse, the sperm produced can enter into the female and fertilize the female's egg, which can lead to the creation of an embryo.

The process is initiated when the male becomes sexually aroused and excited. The male sperm that is produced in the testicles and has moved to the epididymis so that the sperm can grow and mature will leave the epididymis via the vas deferens and travel to the ampulla where it is combined with other fluids to create the semen. While this is happening, the Cowper's glands have produced a fluid to coat the urethra and protect the sperm as it travels through the penis. At this point, there is a great deal of pelvic thrusting and ejaculation whereby the semen is pushed through the urinary opening. The rhythmic contractions of the muscles near the base of the penis drives the semen out in spurts. The actual amount of volume during ejaculation varies from man to man. It also tends to decrease with age and increase with the length of time between ejaculations. Ejaculation usually produces a tremendous sensation of release because after it occurs, there is a release of muscle tension and a gradual relaxation of the penis. After an ejaculation, the man will then return to what is known as the refractory period between ejaculations. This term refers to the time that is necessary for the body to rest and recuperate before the male can achieve another erection and orgasm again. The refractory period usually gets longer as you get older. However, the periods vary from man to man and the more frequently a man ejaculates, the shorter the in between period is likely to be. The average male will only have an ejaculation orgasm once a day in a 24 hour cycle.

Chapter XII

The Female Sexual Anatomy

The female sexual organs are both inside and outside of the body and are more complex. Thus there is frequently confusion or misunderstanding by both men and women regarding them.

A woman should get a more accurate picture of her body. It is smart to know and understand how the body works and functions. If you have not had the opportunity before, take the time to give yourself a self examination and explore the genital area.

The sexual area between a woman's legs is called the genital area or vulva. The woman has folds of flesh called lips in the genital area. The large outer lips (labia) are known as the labia majora. Inside that is the labia minora or small inner lips that protect the vagina opening. At the top of the small lips is a little bud referred to as the clitoris. The clitoris is extremely sensitive and when it's stimulated it gives her sexual pleasure. When a woman is aroused, the blood vessels in the genital area, clitoris and inner lips swell and her clitoris becomes erect. The woman during an orgasm will have a series of muscle contractions and tension is released.

The organs inside the woman are the vagina, uterus, fallopian tubes and ovaries.

THE FEMALE ANATOMY:

Vulva or genital area:	The external part of the female anatomy between her legs.
Mons veneris:	The layer of fatty tissue that pads the pelvic bone underneath it. It is usually covered with hair.
Clitoral Hood:	The clitoral hood may cover all of the clitoris or just a section of it. It is a layer of skin.
Clitoris:	The sensual pleasure button of a woman. This is a very sensitive organ. Its purpose is that it seems to create a sensation of excitement in a woman. It is very small. When it is touched or aroused it will become enlarged with blood much like a man's penis and become erect.
Vaginal Opening:	The vaginal opening refers to the area where the female's menstrual flow during her period flows out. It is also the opening where a erect penis penetrates during the act of intercourse.
Urethra Opening:	The female urinates from this opening.
Hymen:	Refers to a piece of skin that is either partially or totally covers the vagina opening. It is believed that this delicate membrane indicates whether a person is a virgin or not. In reality, the hymen can become torn during any number of activities, including exercise and masturbation. Even doctors cannot tell for sure if a female has had sex. However, it is kind of a folk lore that if the hymen is in place that a woman is still a virgin. However, medical reports

have shown that because the hymen may be stronger in certain females, that even pregnant females can still have a hymen intact.

Labia Minora: Refers to the small inner lips that protect the vagina opening.

Labia Majora: Refers to the large outer lips that protect the vagina area.

Ovarian Follicles: The compartments that make up the ovaries and that holds the individual ovum until it is ripe and ready to be released.

Ovaries: The two oval shaped structures that hold the female eggs.

Ovum: The tiny eggs that carry the mother's genetic matrix and that become fertilized during intercourse by the male's sperm.

Fallopian Tubes: Fragile, thin tubes that carry the ova to the uterus.

Uterus: A pear shaped hollow muscular organ where the fetus will develop. It is this area that becomes blood enriched during the menstrual cycle and then sheds the enriched tissue during menstruation.

Fimbria: The small, finger-like extensions at the end of the fallopian tubes.

Cervix: This a small opening between the uterus and the vagina. It separates the vagina from the uterus.

Bartholin's Glands: Two small glands that are located inside the walls of the vagina and that have the capability to secrete fluid.

Endometrium: The layer of skin on the uterus that gets thick and falls off during menstruation.

Vagina: The hollow passage way that connects the uterus to the outside of the body. At the vagina opening is the area where the small inner lips, large inner lips and the clitoris are located.

Anus: The opening where the female defecates from.

Female Internal Reproductive System

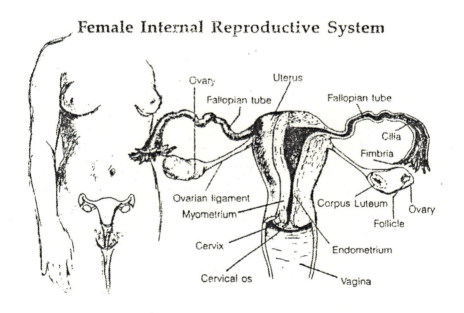

Women in today's society have much more control over their reproductive lives than their predecessors and to a certain extent can plan when to have children. This is a very important fact that can affect the relationship in a positive way. This enables the father to be an active partner in planning and raising the child. This also enables the woman to wait until she finds the right partner so she has both a good husband and father. If your relationship has a good foundation, then having a child together is both an expression of love and a strong bond.

The Breasts

The pair of mammae occurring on the chest usually starts to develop sometime after the age of 12 in a female. This is also the signal that puberty has started. In every culture throughout history more has been written about the anatomy of a woman's breasts than any other feature. It seems to hold a special place in almost any culture and is even associated with fertility in many cultures. Breasts may change in shape and size during the evolvement of the female. The female breast is an important part of the reproductive system because it is made up of numerous milk glands, sometimes called mammary glands. These glands are surrounded by protective fatty tissue. Each breast has a larger darkened area called the areola. This area is very sensitive to both touch and temperature. That is why when it is very cold sometimes the woman's breasts will become very taunt and perky. It is also the area that during sexual gratification will become tender, sensitive and will respond with physical changes. Towards the center of areola is a round nipple. This is a slight protrusion from the tip of the breast and it is where the milk ducts discharge. The milk ducts are inside the breast itself and come up against the chest wall.

A woman's breasts undergo numerous changes during sexual arousal and can be the source of much pleasure and gratification. The nipple erection is usually a sign of sexual arousal and then the areolas will swell because they are becoming engorged with blood. This also makes the nipples and breasts more sensitive to touch.

There are ancient myths about the fountain of life coming from the woman's breast. The breasts are a potential source of sexual pleasure and in some cultures the breasts are revered as a sign of fertility. The breasts have become a symbol for a woman's attraction and the breasts are usually one of the first things that are discussed regarding a woman's physical features. However, no matter the size, shape or texture, the breasts will give the same sexual satisfaction to all women. The Kinsey Institute reports that in a study of men and what they found attractive in a women, half of those studied said they preferred small breasts.

Now that we've reviewed the basic sexual organs and zones of the body, we can discuss in detail the erogenous zones of the body.

Chapter XIII

The Pleasure Zones

The purpose of this section and the following chapters is to provide you with information and techniques to make you a great lover, one capable of experiencing new pleasures. Along with mastering these techniques comes both an understanding and a responsibility.

If you plan on having a completely sexual relationship, then you have a plan for disaster that will leave one or both of you with hurt and emotional scars. Secondly, as you are by now doubtlessly aware, there are risks involved in sexual intimacy. Therefore, it is essential that you find out about your partner's sexual history and practice safe sex until you both have had exams and tests. I know that safe sex is not on your mind when you meet that special person who lights your fire, but the possible life-altering consequences are too great. You must be responsible and put your self and your future before your hormones.

Cardinal Rule

> You are solely responsible for your sexual relationship if it is NOT exciting and pleasurable. You cannot hire a lawyer and sue if it turns out to be poor, disappointing or limp.

The skin, as we've said before, is the largest of all sex organs. Through the nerve endings nestled within our skin we receive all of the pleasurable and delicious messages from touch. The body has many sexual hot spots. Usually these are referred to as erogenous zones, G spots or pleasure spots.

This refers to an area or place that is very sensitive to the kiss, touch or fondle. In fact, there is no part of the human body that is not sufficiently sensitive to affect erotic arousal and in some cases even orgasms.

Dr. Alfred Kinsey did thousands of interviews for his books and he found that some people were so sensitive that merely touching what we consider normal parts of the body like the ear lobes, hands, eyebrows or inner thigh could create sexual excitement and even cause the recipient to reach orgasm. Therefore, you must think of these pleasure zones or erogenous zones as fluid areas of the body that can change from person to person and even vary depending on your partner's mood. That's the joy of exploring each other's body. The most important thing is for you to be sensitive to your partner and find out how and where they like to be touched. Guide your partner, show them how to caress or fondle a part that you enjoy having caressed. In many cases, especially for women, being touched and stroked is an essential prelude to sexual arousement and pleasure and can bring greater enjoyment and satisfaction to the relationship.

Before we begin to describe in detail the different ways and methods to make the body more sensitive for potential sensuous pleasures, we must dismiss many of the false myths regarding foreplay, sexual intercourse and orgasms.

Because of the taboo against open discussion about sexuality, many false rumors and myths have developed regarding intercourse and orgasms. In fact, since so little has been produced regarding the feelings and sensations that one experiences during an orgasm, some people do not realize for many years whether or not they are having an orgasm or what to expect in a sexual relationship. In many cultures, even today, sex is used chiefly for procreation rather than for pleasure. Women are expected to perform for their husbands and men feel it is their duty or obligation. Therefore, unfortunately, many couples today never experience the true enjoyment, pleasure or reward of a good, healthy, natural sexual relationship.

"A large penis will give greater sexual satisfaction to a woman."

This is a completely unfounded myth.

"A female who does not have orgasms on a regular basis will be unable to have an orgasm when she wants."

Again, this is a completely unfounded and untrue statement.

"An orgasm for a woman is triggered only when the penis penetrates in a strong and hard thrusting manner in the vagina."

This may or may not bring about an orgasm for some women. Many women, as we'll explain later, are not receptive to this type of action. Another myth is that a woman can only experience an orgasm when the penis has penetrated the vagina. This is completely unfounded.

"You must concentrate to have good sexual intercourse and an orgasm."

Actually, trying too hard may create anxiety and frustration and thus prohibit the person from relaxing enough to fully enjoy the situation and experience an orgasm.

A woman may have difficulty in reaching an orgasm because she has not been properly stimulated and aroused sexually. This does not mean that she should fake it however. Faking an orgasm in order to make your partner feel good can make the problem worse. It can give you feelings of inadequacy, anxiety and frustration which will continue to cause you additional problems in future contact. Secondly, it may create a feeling of mistrust in the man once he is aware that you're faking it. This is not a good practice and over a period of time will leave you feeling drained and shallow, taking away the real spirit of enjoyment and companionship.

Lubricants and Their Application

Throughout the following sections of the book we will be referring to lubricants. Lubricants come in two categories. The first category are lubricants that contain spermicide known as Nonoxynol-9. The spermicides in this category are used as contraceptives because they will eliminate the effect of the male sperm on the female egg. Some medical tests have revealed that spermicide, especially ones containing Nonoxynol-9, are effective in reducing the chance of infection from certain sexually transmitted diseases. The second category of lubricants come in a variety of consistencies. Water-based, oil-based, scented, colored, unscented, clear, liquids, gels, flavored. They are primarily for two purposes. First, to create greater sensitivity while having sexual contact and secondly, to add fun and excitement to the experience.

When we recommend spermicides, we're recommending them to address concerns of protection. When we are recommending a lubricant, such as a flavored lubricant, we are recommending it to enhance the sensitivity and enjoyment of your sexual activities.

Never use oil-based lubricants with a latex condom as such lubricants will destroy its integrity. Oil-based lubricants wreck latex condoms and therefore eliminate their protection against pregnancy and sexually transmitted diseases.

The only use for oil-based lubricants is when you are using them for the body rubs or the manual stimulation that we will discuss in the other sections. However, it is preferred to always have on hand water-based lubricants. Therefore, you avoid ever making a mistake at the wrong time or in a moment of heated passion.

When purchasing a lubricant, read the label and see what ingredients are listed. Determine whether it is an oil-based or water-based product. Also, be mindful to look for any ingredients that you or your partner might be allergic to. Be wary of any silicone based lubricants. These products are made with Dimethicone, offer no protective value, and are designed for external use only.

There are a large number of lubricants on the market today. Some have a slight taste. Some are colorless. Some are odorless. You can usually find a pretty good variety at a drugstore or even a supermarket. There are also some lubricants on the market today that you can use for manual stimulation or for body rubs that create a warm tingly feeling. Such products can certainly add a lot of excitement and spice to a sexual encounter. Some of them come in flavors. Most convey an exotic, tingly feeling when they are applied to certain areas like the inner thighs, head of the penis, testicles, nipples, breasts or small of the back.

I have included in the back of the book a chart listing the different varieties of lubricants, including their brand names and characteristics, for your reference and use. However, part of the fun of a sexual relationship is the anticipation and exploration. So you may wish to go to your local store and review the products yourself and read all the different characteristics and claims they make. The important thing to keep in mind is the product's specific use. It's vital to know whether it's for sensitivity and enjoyment or for protection. You need to know for certain whether it's for internal or external use and if it can be used with a latex condom.

In several parts of the book we talk about sensual fantasies and sexual techniques where we employ things like chocolate and caramel to different parts of the body and either lick or suck it off. These substances are not to interpreted as being lubricants or of providing any form of protection. There are a variety of very exotic and enjoyable items on the market today that you can pick up. Some come in unbelievable flavors and our old friend, chocolate, which women love and is also a natural aphrodisiac, comes in a variety of things like jars or tubes. They need to be warmed either in a microwave or with body heat. The sensation they create is fantastic. However a lot of these are to be use only for sensuality and never to be used as a lubricant or in conjunction with a latex condom, because the oils and ingredients in some of these items will effect a latex condom.

Applying the different massage oils or lubricants can be a sexual experience in and of itself. It is certainly very sensuous to take and caress in a light feathery stoking manner different parts of the body while giving a very gentle, soothing massage. In this case, both the lubricants and the oils enhance sensitivity while also stimulating the other senses. As we said, many of them have certain fragrances and ingredients that will add to the enjoyment, either giving a slight warming or a tingling sensation to the body. Some of these massage oils can be picked up at beauty shops or salons or where fine oils and creams are sold.

A number of women have raved that a very sensuous, excellent technique for foreplay is to have a man pour a generous amount of massage oil or lubricant over their breasts and then slowly rub the oil around the torso and the breasts. This creates a sensation of arousal for both, especially if time and care is taken to find out the exact areas that are most sensitive to touch and cause the greatest stimulation. The obvious reverse is for a woman to take an oil or lubricant and apply it to her partner. Starting with the man's inner thighs, the woman should sensuously work her fingers around the genital areas to massage and rub the thighs, testicles and penis. This can be extremely tantalizing and teasing to the man.

The Pleasure Spots

Certain parts of the anatomy, like the nipples, tongue, clitoris and glans, are commonly known as pleasure zones because they are more richly endowed with nerve endings and thus respond to touch more than most body areas. However, as we will illustrate, all the way from the tips of your toes to the ends of your earlobes, a certain caress, touch, or light feathery brush can produce sufficient sensitivity to sexually arouse your partner.

In fact, the late Dr. Alfred Kinsey observed among 12,000 people that he interviewed that some women could reach orgasm simply by the kissing or fondling of their earlobes. A few men could reach orgasm if a lover kissed their nipples, and several women could actually climax through the stroking of their eyebrows.

Variety is the spice of a sexual relationship. Learn to explore. As we discussed before, learn to communicate with your partner, not only verbally, but through touch. Pay attention to their responses and try to learn exactly what it is that triggers an orgasm for them. It may be difficult at first, but work with your partner. Ask them to point or move your hand to the place that gives them the greatest sensation and pleasure. Not all the methods we will discuss will bring about the same sexual responses in men and women. You have to test and explore what are the most sensitive and responsive areas and techniques to use with your partner.

A sensual prelude to sexual intercourse is what is commonly called foreplay. Most women enjoyed being touched, kissed and fondled, especially if done with a gentle and loving caress. The rewards and benefits for both partners are numerous because it will arouse and stimulate the woman to higher levels thus bringing about greater enjoyment and intimacy for both.

For the woman, the clitoris is one of the strongest hot spots, both the head and the shaft of the clitoris are highly responsive to the touch. Be careful. Do not be too rough because this part of the woman's anatomy is so tender that in some women it can also create pain and discomfort. So go gently, then watch her responses and you will know how to proceed.

The exotic and sensuous feelings that massaging the clitoris can bring about are tremendous. They have been described as a frenzied, frantic feeling. During an orgasm a women might feel a drastic increase in heart rate, light headedness, or have a series of involuntary muscle spasms. Some may feel many things and some may feel things differently, but it is certain that proper stimulation will arouse the woman to new heights.

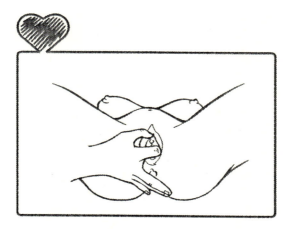

The small inner lips of the genitals are richly supplied with nerves, especially on the inside, and touching and caressing of this area can bring about exotic arousal. Dr. Kinsey's studies show that many women will get as much or the same sensation of the stimulation of this area as the clitoris.

The first several inches of the vaginal opening are rich with nerve endings. Naturally, this area is quite sensitive.

Hot Spot—The Inner Lipshe elusive G spot, that area know for sensuous pleasures, is a small area on the upper wall of the vagina. The tissue in this area is surrounded by bracteal tissue like part of the penis is, and during sexual stimulation will swell making it even more sensitive. This spot can be found directly behind the pubic bone, in the upper front wall of the vagina, about 2" inside the opening. Although the exact size and location varies, it is usually found about half way between the back of the pubic bone and the front of the cervix near the neck of the bladder. This is where intimacy is very helpful because the woman can describe and guide her partner to where the exact location is that gives her the most sensation and pleasure. Even the best lovers at times need a helping hand.

Some women respond very quickly to the kissing and fondling of their breasts and nipples. However, for some the stimulation in these areas may not lead to immediate arousal because they are so tender that their lover's touch actually brings about discomfort or even pain. This again is an individual situation that must be handled differently from person to person. However, in many cases, women will enjoy a tender fondling, caressing and kissing of the breast and nipples. The woman's breast usually goes through a change during sexual excitement. The may become stiff and perky, which usually is the first sign of arousal. Although not all women will get erect nipples, after a while, the breasts themselves will swell and become even more sensitive. Different things will create sexual arousement in a woman. Sometimes kissing of the nipple, the gentle massaging of the nipple with the lips, or rubbing your tongue along the nipple and sides will cause flutters and tingling. Sometimes massaging the nipple gently is stimulating. Most women like to have their breasts fondled during sex and foreplay. The main thing is not to feel inhibited and to ask your partner what she enjoys.

Breasts are a pleasure zone for both women and men. The key is to let your partner know where and how you want to be touched so that in the future they can please you during your lovemaking.

During the foreplay time, many areas can become even more sensitive than in normal times. For example, the earlobes become engorged with blood during sex, sometimes even noticeably swelling. For some, they become intensely sensitive to touch. Often, the gentle kissing, rubbing or caressing of the inner ears and the earlobes can be a very effective turn on.

The inner surface of the thigh is richly endowed with nerve endings. Glancing your fingers lightly across this area can generate a high level of sexual arousal for many. Another often over looked erogenous zone is the foot. The toes and the soles of the feet are extremely sensitive to a light touch or a massage. Try working your hands along the small of your lover's back, continuing the motion down to her buttocks. Rub her using a light, gentle, scratching caress. This massaging rub can bring about sensuous pleasures and a tingling feeling. Of course, the mouth, lips and tongue are the most noticeable and first used areas during foreplay. You can start with a gentle peck, progress with a caressing of your lover's lips, and finally give into your passions with a French kiss.

The area between the anus and the genitals in some men and women is extremely sensitive. In fact, a gentle stroking of this area with some pressure applied at a point about midway between the anus and scrotum will cause sensual arousal and an erection in men.

Even the arms, palms and fingers of some become sensitive to the touch and cause sexual arousement and excitement when they are caressed. If you find that your lover has sensitive hands, then take the initiative with some creative foreplay. Trace circles with your tongue around their palms, suck at their fingers.

The genital area of the female, since it's comprised of many parts, is extremely sensitive to the touch, more so than most men realize. If you perform oral sex on the female it is usually best done slowly, gently and lovingly. Try gently massaging the clitoris with your tongue while your fingers stroke the walls of the small lips around the vagina. This area can generate a great deal of sexual arousal. When fondling your partner's more sensitive areas, move slowly and gently at first. Let your partner tell you how she feels and if she is becoming turned on.

From interviews done in clinical studies, it's clear that most men usually are very fast and rough when caressing a woman. However, most women find it more pleasurable if the man moves in a slow, easy and gentle way. This is especially true when the man inserts his fingers or thumb into the vagina. It is a gentle stroking of the clitoris that brings about the more favorable responses. Again, your partner can guide you as to what is the appropriate method and rhythm. Some women do enjoy a greater pressure and quickness which stimulates them and arouses them to a greater sexual peak. However, this is a very personal thing and you want your partner to enjoy it, so let your partner's reaction guide you. Be attentive to what pleases her so that she can be attentive to what pleases you.

Many of the same areas of the body are sensitive and pleasurable in the man as they are in the woman. However, just as in the woman's unique genital area, the man has certain hot spots in his genital area as well. Usually the area underneath and just behind the glans or the head of the penis is the most sensitive spot. A gentle, caressing or rubbing of this area usually brings about sexual arousement.

The coronal ridge, which is the rim of the glans, is very responsive to touch and caressing.

The penis itself is sensitive to the touch. If you move your hand gently down the penis, stroking it, the man will usually become sexually aroused. Once the penis becomes erect, the foreskin retracts and the penis is hard. It will actually change color in many men because it is so engorged with blood. You can massage the penis with your hand, tongue or you can move it with your hand back from the testicles. This bottom shaft of the penis is a sensitive area and rubbing it with your hand or stroking it in a fast manner with your tongue will cause sexual arousement. One of the most pleasurable ways for a woman to arouse her man is to lick the tip of his penis, then wrap her lips over the head. The woman should then continue moving her mouth from the head further on down the shaft, then back up to the head again. Each repetition of this motion will increase the arousal level of the man, eventually to the point of causing an orgasm.

The woman shouldn't be afraid to let her partner guide her as to the firmness, pressure and speed that is most pleasurable for him. Usually one can see if they're on the right track or not from their partner's breathing patterns or muscle responses. Many times the pelvic area will start a rhythmic contraction much like in intercourse.

Some men are more sensitive than others regarding the breast and nipple area. Some men enjoy having their nipples stimulated during sex play, either by a gentle rubbing with the hand or by a kissing of the lips. Some men enjoy having the woman rub her breasts over his chest and nipples. This will cause a pleasant sensation and, in some cases, sexual arousement.

Research seems to indicate that compared to men, women tend to be less focused on the generals and more sensitive to the entire body's potential for sensuous pleasure.

From survey results, women indicate that they enjoy being touched and stroked all over and that foreplay is a necessary prelude to sexual intercourse.

Everyone has sexual fantasies during their lifetime. Often times these fantasies involve things that would be considered unusual, unnatural, or maybe even taboo. **However, the mind is the body's most fertile erogenous zone and can cause extreme sexual stimulation. So, confide in your partner about your sexual fantasies and desires and together discuss and perhaps explore them. You will soon find out if the reality measures up to the fantasy.** Do not feel guilty or embarrassed about discussing such thoughts. Sometimes it is necessary for some people to live out their fantasies to find out what true and pleasurable sex is and realize that it may not be necessary to have some exotic fantasy in order to enjoy themselves. In other cases it might turn out that the fantasy will create a bona fide climax solely through the exotic use of the partners' minds in living out the fantasy.

Cardinal Rule

> Being honest and intimate with you partner is the easiest way to trigger romantic fantasies because you create a sense of rapport that you are both experiencing together. This will stimulate your partner's romantic fantasies.

Exploration by two mature, consenting adults is the only way to find the areas of stimulation and pleasure that will bring about the arousing sensuous feelings that you desire. Since the skin is so richly endowed with nerves, and a person's mind can conjure up almost any fantasy, it is up to you to explore the frontiers of your lover's flesh and hot spots.

So What is an Orgasm?

An orgasm is a whole body response that creates a variety of wonderful feelings. However, no one in the medical field has a complete understanding of exactly what triggers an orgasm or the sensations that an orgasm creates in each individual. Does an orgasm actually originate as a result of the stimulation of the sexual organs or is an orgasm caused by the emotional stimulation of the mind? The whole process is not very clear. However, what is clear is that an orgasm gives an unequal pleasure for both men and women. Orgasms are the climax of the sex act. They create a feeling of sudden, intense pleasure that is usually accompanied by an increase in pulse rate and blood pressure. Both men and women will experience involuntary spasms in the pelvic muscles. Women will feel vaginal contractions while men will ejaculate. It is an intense but fleeting moment. The orgasm is an individual experience, and is unique for each person. Usually people will not respond to the same stimuli in the same way. An orgasm in some can cause trembling, shaking, a sense of explosion, a frenzied sex drive, an increase in heart rate, a relaxed, relieved sensation, or a tingling and flushed feeling all over the body. However and whatever the individual experiences during orgasms, it is a sexual climax that is reached as a result of sexual stimuli.

An orgasm is a build up of sexual excitement and a release of energy that reaches a peak or climax and causes a wonderful and pleasing sensation. This is the result of a normal orgasm. However, if one of the partners is having difficulty and does not experience a pleasant sensation, it is usually because intercourse involves some pain or distress from a physical problem. It could be as simple as the female's vagina not being well lubricated. This can be source of discomfort for both men and women. It is necessary to understand your partner and be intimate with them. Discuss how they like to be touched and if they are experiencing the proper sensation. This is another reason why it is important to learn to properly stimulate each other in order for each partner to relax and be in the correct emotional state to experience a complete, exciting and satisfying orgasm.

Women are able to have more than one orgasm in a short period of time. It is very common for a woman to have an orgasm at a different time then the man. However, the sensation and time spent together is as rewarding and pleasurable to both parties. A woman's orgasm may cause her entire body to shake. She might feel her vagina, uterus, hips and back throb and almost quiver. Thus, the woman may be in a position to experience the sensation of an orgasm more than once during a physical encounter, especially if the female has been both emotionally and physically stimulated prior to intercourse. This will also help induce multiple orgasms. The man should practice with his partner to learn how to relax and stimulate his partner in a pleasurable way. This will pay big rewards and benefits for both in the enjoyment and satisfaction of sexual contact. For this reason, foreplay is very important. A sexually active person should strive to be sensitive to their partner's needs and responses. One of the most common mistakes made by men is that they rush into sexual intercourse before the female is fully relaxed, ready and lubricated. Thus, one of the common comments from women is that the whole sexual interplay is over before they have had an opportunity to really enjoy it. This is also one of the major reasons why women do not experience orgasms with each sexual encounter. Not all orgasms are the same for each person. Furthermore, they rarely occur spontaneously for a woman. A man needs to properly relax his partner both mentally and physically first. He shouldn't rush into penetration, but instead should stimulate her through touching, caressing and kissing. The environment one is in makes a difference as well. The thoughtful lover will take the time to set up a romantic or erotic atmosphere. The excitement and pleasure may not be as great for the female if an encounter is rushed, thus reducing her chances at achieving an orgasm.

The key component to having a good orgasm is for both partners to be relaxed, consenting and properly stimulated. If either one of the partners has anxiety over being touched or having intercourse, they will not experience the full sensations of excitement and satisfaction. It is very important that the key elements and components of a good sexual relationship are in place and that the partners are not experiencing guilt or anxiety over what they are doing. If you perceive that your partner is having difficulty or is apprehensive, then you must discuss it and work through the steps or guidelines that are in *Book Two: Coping with the Anxiety of a Sexual Relationship*.

Cardinal Rule

> The Hite Report on male sexuality revealed that women feel cheated and frustrated when they don't have a climax and the male does. Also, the report revealed that most men did *not* know how to bring a woman to orgasm and furthermore that most women didn't feel right to tell this fact to the man while having sex.

Medical studies and surveys have revealed that many women have trouble reaching orgasms consistently. In fact, many married women who said they were happily married had trouble becoming aroused or achieving consistent or multiple orgasms. If this is the case, it is not recommended that the woman "fake" an orgasm in order to make her partner feel good. It is necessary to have, as we have discussed, honesty and intimacy in a relationship and good communication. The woman must confide in her partner that she isn't experiencing the sensation she desires. In turn, the man should be willing to pay close attention to her responses in order to try to learn what it is that precisely stimulates her and triggers an orgasm.

Cardinal Rule

> Most women do not reach orgasm during normal sexual intercourse. Therefore, to heighten the women's enjoyment, you and your partner should practice new techniques and positions to find out what increases her enjoyment.

The trouble with faking an orgasm is twofold. It may have an adverse affect on your partner. Once they find out, it will make them feel inadequate or distrustful. This can weaken the relationship and eventually cause a person to become burned out on sex because they are not deriving both mental and physical pleasure from the contact.

If the female is having difficulty reaching an orgasm because she is not properly stimulated, the male should try what is called coital alignment. That is a technique in which the man rides high when he is entering the woman so that his pubic bone directly stimulates her clitoris by rocking back and forth against it. The man should also take his time and try to avoid a lot of deep thrusts so that he can properly stimulate the woman. This allows her to become lubricated so that she is fully relaxed, enjoys the contact, becomes satisfied and they both reach an exciting orgasm and climax.

Coital Alignment

Women should take over the responsibility for and control of her own stimulation if she does not have an orgasm. The following section will describe explicit techniques, but only you know your body and pleasure spots best so guide your partner and use the positions that give you the best stimulation and satisfaction.

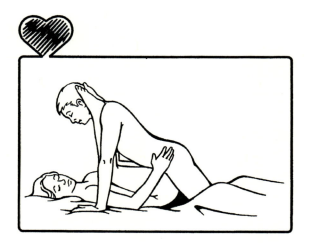

Masters and Johnson's research discovered one major difference between men and women when experiencing an orgasm. Usually after an orgasm, a man's erection will wilt and he will slip into a state of sexual unresponsiveness known as the "refractory period." This can last anywhere from a few minutes to a day or more. However, women have the capability of having multiple orgasms. They are responsive to additional stimuli and sensation and can continue to experience orgasms. Dr. Masters has stated, "The female has an infinitely greater capacity for sexual response than a man ever dreamed of."

The last phase (refractory phase) of an orgasm is similar in nature for most men and women. You have a total feeling or sense of intimacy, closeness, release, and relaxation. Many times, the couple will feel like cuddling and falling asleep together or just having their own space and gently falling asleep.

Cardinal Rule

To be a sensitive lover you must respect your lover's needs and feelings. Learn how to please him or her, and don't be afraid to ask them for help.

Chapter XIV

What Women Really Want

Extraordinary Foreplay

Foreplay for many can be even more enjoyable and rewarding than intercourse itself. It's like having dessert before the entree. The secret of foreplay is learning to communicate, both verbally and by touch. Let your partner know what feels good, and in turn find out what makes them feel good. Learn how to sooth and relax each other. You already know from the prior sections the wonderful magic of touching and the enjoyment and stimulation that it can bring.

Foreplay is an essential building block in a good sexual relationship and to having the ultimate orgasm. When you arouse your partner, many times the anticipation and excitement you experience before sex is more pleasurable than the climax you reach during. Always keep in mind the body's hotspots and the techniques needed to stimulate them.

The key to good foreplay is to be intimate and honest with your partner and let them know what turns you on. Be willing to experiment and learn through the secret of touch what arouses your partner. Let them know what pleases you and remain sensitive to their needs. Men have to learn to be more patient and understanding. A man needs to be sensitive to the responses of a woman, to her impulses and her needs. Many times men more than women have to learn to listen, to be verbal and to be attentive. Sometimes it is not as necessary to be verbal as it is to be sensitive and honest in your intimacy. You can guide your mate's actions, movements or hands in such a way to show them what it is that pleases you and how to do it. Finally, we must learn to release the anxiety that we all have of being nervous or scared, the fear that we might do something to embarrass ourselves or our partner. What takes place between the two of you is not being judged or held up against a measuring scale. What is important is what satisfies you and brings enjoyment into your relationship. You cannot make a mistake. You are simply experimenting, developing and honing your talents with your mate.

It is entirely possible that the pleasure and enjoyment you receive from foreplay can last for many hours, even all day. During an extended period of time, both partners will be able to experience extreme pleasure and satisfaction, multiple orgasms and a sense of closeness that they cannot experience in any other way.

Cardinal Rule

Intercourse is only one dish in the sweet banquet of love. Don't think it's the whole meal!

In the Hite Report, a study of female sexuality by author Shere Hite, it was disclosed that many time during intercourse women aren't stimulated enough to reach orgasm. Therefore, it is especially important to be sensitive to your partner's needs and to engage in the proper touching and foreplay so as to both physically stimulate her as well as mentally excite her. It may even be more pleasurable to both parties to sexually stimulate her sufficiently so she has an orgasm prior to having intercourse. You should make this part of your ritual of lovemaking if the woman is not responsive during intercourse. This can be more satisfying and enjoyable for both partners and create the same sensation of satisfaction and enjoyment that can be experienced through intercourse.

Hite's work has been monumental in helping both researchers and the public at large understand the responses and trends in the sexuality of both men and women. Her work looks at traditional concepts of sexuality from a completely new perspective. From the extensive research and surveys that Hite and her staff conducted, we now realize that **approximately 70% of women do not have orgasms from intercourse, but do have them from more direct clitoral stimulation. This one fact puts a whole new light on the importance of foreplay and how a woman will perceive a sexual relationship.** The following is an excerpt from the Cheryl Hite report on women as revolutionary agents of change:

> ...not only were women tired of the old mechanical pattern of penetration, intercourse and ejaculation, but many also found that always having to have intercourse, knowing you will have intercourse as a foregone conclusion, is mechanical and boring. If you know in advance that intercourse has to be a part of every heterosexual sexual encounter, there is almost no way the old mechanical pattern of sexual relations can be avoided, since intercourse usually leads to male orgasm, which signals the end of (sex).

Cardinal Rule

> A common myth among men is that hard penetration and heavy thrusting will stimulate the woman to have an orgasm. The Hite research, Master and Johnson research and numerous other research programs have proven this myth to be completely false. Only in a very small percentage of women does this type of intercourse bring about an orgasm and satisfaction.

A lot of women will have intercourse with the man they love because they feel obligated to have it, or they want to please him. However, the real man of all seasons will realize that it should be the choice of the woman whether or not to have intercourse, and it should be a pleasurable form of sexual contact. You can create the right mood, feeling and desire by practicing the techniques that we are discussing in the next section as well as in the prior section. Relaxation, caressing, kissing and extensive foreplay will open a whole new horizon of pleasurable sex for both genders and will allow in many cases the female to reach new levels of sensation and excitement.

If the man is normally quick to climax, then he should take the time to engage in enough foreplay for the woman to orgasm before or quickly after penetration. Again, intimacy and honesty are necessary. The woman needs to guide the man and inform him when she feels ready for penetration. The man must be sensitive enough to understand and appreciate both the responses and the needs of the woman. The time spent together will be a turn on for both parties if they are sensitive to each other responses and needs.

Through extraordinary foreplay, the couple will dramatically increase the sensation, excitement and enjoyment that they experience together. This will also create a much stronger bonding between the two. If they are mutually happy and satisfied and enjoy their time together, they will be brought closer together and over a period of time the bonding will become stronger and stronger, which is one of the main goals of a good sexual relationship.

Cardinal Rule

> Foreplay will increase the odds of the woman climaxing during intercourse. You need to stimulate the clitoris to the point that she feels an orgasm is imminent, then get into your favorite position for intercourse.

Men usually want sex and then feel intimate. Women feel intimate and then want sex. Foreplay is the bridge between a man and woman's sexual wants.

Great Foreplay Gives Great Rewards

The pattern of male erection, male penetration, and male orgasm frustrates and emotionally hurts a lot of women because many times this leaves only the male satisfied. Many women want men to learn and appreciate the subtleties of good sex and gain an appreciation for each other's bodies.

Cardinal Rule

> Women need to be teachers if their lover is inept at foreplay or sexual stimulation. The man wants to please and it supercharges his ego when he knows his woman has achieved pleasure. The woman needs to help him become a fantastic lover—by guiding, showing, telling and, if necessary, by controlling him. Ultimately, both partners will share in the ecstasies.

Great foreplay creates anticipation, desire and prolongs the feeling of pleasure and satisfaction. Foreplay starts the engine revving, the juices flowing, and raises anticipation levels higher and higher. Thus once a really enjoyable sexual encounter and climax have been obtained, it will create even deeper feelings of pleasure and satisfaction. It is unfortunate that so much of the material in movies and books has concentrated on quickly achieving an orgasm. A quick orgasm is not the true or ultimate sexual encounter. A satisfying sexual encounter should leave both partners in a pleasurable, fulfilled, satisfied state of utopia and relaxation.

Good foreplay should include a build up of intensity using the techniques that we've described. Kissing can start the passion between two lovers, as can touching, caressing and hugging. Put your hands on the bare skin of your partner in a firm, almost lightly scratching manner. Using this technique, search the body from the toes to the earlobes and find out what points create the greatest sensation and relaxation in your partner. The gentle scratching motion over one's thighs, back, shoulders or legs can generate an electric, tingly feeling that starts the nerves vibrating with anticipation. Use your lips and tongue to explore the different crevices of the body. Blow warm, sweet breaths across the ears, nipples and genital areas. In a smooth, rhythmic way, stroke the hairs in the pubic area while kissing and sucking on the breasts and nipples. Now is the time to employ not only technique, but creativity as well. Try delicately massaging the clitoris. Remember, as it swells it gains sensitivity. It would probably be desirable to use one of the lubricants that we've discussed. Pour some into the palm of your hands. Gently rub your hands together to warm up the lubricant and then, in a light but firm manner, start to massage and stimulate the clitoris. The woman can return the favor by rubbing the shaft of her partner's penis with a rhythmic motion. Any of these acts will increase anticipation, desire and sensitivity.

Since the sexual climax is such a tremendous release of energy, it involves as we've described many parts of the body and produces many side effects such as muscle spasms, pulsation and at times almost unbearable pleasure. All of this is magnified through the heightened sensitivity of the penis, vagina and the clitoris so that when they eventually come together they are stimulated and sensitive to the point that they can fully receive each other. They are almost in a sense supercharged with sensitivity and are primed to have an unbelievable, sensational orgasm, one that envelops the whole body.

Female Orgasm

Every woman is different. What is pleasurable and exciting for one may not even be a turn on for another. However, the following techniques are almost foolproof. When applied properly, they can have a dramatically pleasing, stimulating effect on a woman. If the stimulation occurs long enough, the sensational tingling feeling will eventually give way to an eruption of pleasure, climaxing in a tremendous, mind blowing orgasm. These same techniques can be used of course in foreplay to prepare the woman so that she is filled with anticipation and is well lubricated and ready to receive the penetration of the penis, thereby allowing the heightened and intimate experience of two people having a simultaneous sexual climax and orgasm.

I recommend that you lightly lubricate your hands and fingers for this technique. You may even want to pour a little lubricant into your woman's belly button and use it as a little reservoir to occasionally dip your fingers into. In the section on female anatomy we explained and defined that many of the very sensitive hot spots in a woman are located around the clitoris, the inner lips and the first few inches of the vagina. The idea is to cause arousal in the woman by properly stimulating all of these areas simultaneously.

With your fingers and thumb lubricated rub your index finger along the inner front upper wall of the vagina from inside, angling towards the pelvic bone and clitoris. At the same time use your thumb to gently massage the clitoris. With your third or fourth finger, rub or tickle the perineum area, the area below the vagina and the large outer lips. Or, if your woman prefers, you can take your third finger and stimulate the opening of the anus. Once you reach a sort of rhythmic motion you will be able to tell by her sighs and responses how much stimulation and pressure you should apply. Each woman will require her own particular rhythm and pressure until you get to the right tempo, which will create a tingling, exciting build up of energy. If you continue it will manifest in an explosion of a sexual climax and orgasm. Or if you so desire, you can build up to a heightened point of stimulation and anticipation and then each of you can experience a sexual climax and orgasm together when the male has penetrated the female.

Another exciting and unusual technique is to lubricate both hands and place the palms together with both index fingers going in and out of the vagina, stimulating the lips and the inner walls of the vagina. At the same time the two thumbs work in harmony on stimulating the clitoris. The third and fourth fingers are devoted to caressing the perineum area.

This form of stimulation will create a heightened sexual sensitivity. The woman will be so enraptured with sexual pleasure that she'll either orgasm from the motion of the fingers or beg for intercourse.

You should be reminded at this point that women are very capable of multiple orgasms in a short period of time. Therefore you may wish to stimulate her in foreplay so she will receive full gratification and orgasm. Continue the foreplay until you heighten the level of sensitivity in the clitoris and vagina, then enter her and time it so that you both climax simultaneously. As we said, great foreplay has great rewards for both.

Cardinal Rule

Increase the stimulation by combining an oral technique with a hand technique.

Stimulate the clitoris by hand while the penis has penetrated the vagina so that the woman can have a climax during intercourse.

Cardinal Rule

The woman's clitoris is a pleasure organ. It's only function is to give the woman pleasure. It has nothing to do with procreation. Learn to use it to give her pleasure.

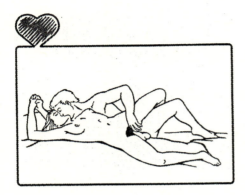

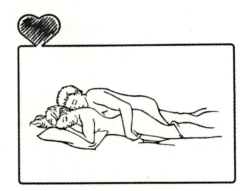

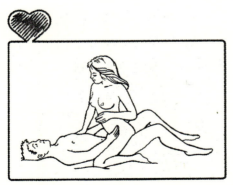

Techniques to stimulate the clitoris while having intercourse so that the woman can have a pleasurable orgasm.

Chapter XV

Sexual Oral Ecstasy

When a man or woman performs oral sex on their partner, they are supercharging the sexual experience. The brain kicks in first. Often the anticipation of the act releases adrenaline and arouses the sex organs. Obviously, even just the thought of receiving oral sex can be very stimulating.

Each partner receives sexual excitement through the act. Every sense is utilized during oral sex. The lovers come into contact with the other's genitalia in the most intimate of manners. Oral sex is a pleasure in and of itself and can set up an even more pleasurable intercourse.

Oral sex is wholesome. The vagina is a self cleaning organ and is free of harmful bacteria. The penis is normally clean and semen is free from any bacteria. Partners should plan ahead and wash or bath in order to relax and really enjoy each other.

The way to add excitement and anticipation to a relationship as well as jump starting sexual sensitivity is through oral sex.

Intimate Communication

One of the building steps of a relationship is to be honest and have intimate communication regarding your feelings and desires. So too, when it comes to sexual enjoyment. You must learn to communicate and take your lover's hand and guide it to the location where you feel it will give you the desired sensation. Do not be afraid to show him or her how to apply pressure, squeeze, hold firmly, caress or fondle the areas that you so desire. In this way you enhance the relationship for both. There is as much joy in seeing the response as in feeling the sensation.

Cardinal Rule

> Creating pleasure and seeing that you are giving pleasure to another builds up one's ego and desire to continue to please.

Prelude to Oral Sex

The most intriguing, sensuous and intimate sex involves oral sex. However, it's a topic that many are nervous or shy about. It is also one of the most talked about topics in group discussions. People not only want to know more about oral sex, but they also want to improve their skill at it. Oral sex is very provocative and can be enticing as well as addictive. Skillfully performing oral sex is one of the best ways to enhance foreplay and create the anticipation and excitement that each lover should have before having intercourse.

Men especially are poor at giving directions, preferences or even acting as a guide when it comes to sexual techniques. That may be why oral sex sometimes is so mysterious and exciting for men, because they are in search of something yet to be experienced. Once they've had really good oral sex, they may become continuously desirous of it, even to the point of addiction.

Some women have difficulty performing oral sex because they feel awkward. In many cases they simply haven't had the opportunity to properly learn how to do it or to practice. They have a great deal of anxiety. This anxiety can create fear and tension, which will destroy both the mood and sensation. You will see from the definitions and illustrations that we have put in this section that there are a great variety of techniques. You have to become familiar and comfortable with those techniques that feel best for you. You can create the excitement and stimulation that you want. A woman shouldn't feel apprehensive about choking or gagging. Many oral sex techniques don't involve taking the entire penis into the mouth and throat, but rather focus on what can be done with the tongue and lips. A great deal of what you have seen and heard in movies regarding oral sex simply is not true. Many sex acts depicted in the media are shown because they are sensational, not because they are stimulating or pleasurable.

Cardinal Rule

Whether or not a woman while performing oral sex swallows the semen is her preference and has absolutely nothing to do with the sensation or pleasure that she is giving her lover when he has an orgasm.

A number of women in discussion groups have expressed at times concerns about whether or not they should swallow the semen during ejaculation. In all the research that's been done, it's been shown that swallowing or having the penis in the mouth during ejaculation has nothing to do with the pleasure, enjoyment or sensation that's created by oral sex. So, it is merely up to the preference of the woman. It will have no bearing if you follow the techniques of creating the desired stimulation, anticipation and excitement during oral sex.

Oral Sex: the Ecstasies

Both men and women fantasize from a very early age about having sex, especially oral sex. With a minimal amount of time and effort, any man or woman can learn new ways to enflame the sparks of passion within their lover.

Here are some general suggestions for enhancing oral sex:

- Make it your idea. Make the first suggestion, gesture or movement. Many times this will reduce the anxiety and nervousness in both parties. To really enjoy sex, you must be relaxed and have anticipation of what will come. That is what creates a lot of the sensation and pleasure.
- Remember that you can always utilize other stimulating techniques while performing oral sex. Just because you're using your mouth doesn't mean that the rest of your body can't get in on the act. Your hands can be especially useful in heightening pleasure, and can be used to give your mouth a break while maintaining the rhythm of ecstasy along your partner's sex organs.
- If you have difficulty performing oral sex, then utilize one of the other techniques such as hand manipulation or body stimulation. Most of the time your lover won't even realize it. They will just think this is a continuation of the same thing to the next level.
- While performing oral sex, if it becomes awkward, try to breathe a little easier and shift your positions. Move around until it is more comfortable and natural. Many times a position change can make a big difference. Be aware of your lover and the signals that they are sending to you. Always be mindful of whether you are causing your partner pain or pleasure. The one thing you do not want to do is create an awkward, bad experience that will make your partner have anxiety the next time. Go slowly and gently until both of you are comfortable and in sync.

Oral Sex on Men

The key to giving good oral sex to a man is for the woman to perform using her mouth, tongue and hands. It is impossible and unnatural for a woman to encompass a man's entire penis in her mouth. As we've defined in the anatomy section, most of the nerve endings and stimuli in a woman are around the edge of the vagina and the clitoris. The same is true for a man. Most of his nerve endings and points of sensation are on the head of the penis and or on the ring just below it. This is the area that you really want to work on and stimulate. The woman should use whichever hand is more comfortable for her. Having a hand on the penis enables her more freedom of motion working on the head and the beginning of the shaft as well as creating a warm comfortable sensation along the shaft of the penis. Many men don't realize that their woman hasn't taken the entire penis into her mouth. They get the sensation of it because she is incorporating the proper use of the hands. Her grip is like a ring around the penis. It forms a tube. This in conjunction with her lips and mouth accommodate the entire penis. However the hand will act as monitor and will determine how far down the lips go along the head and shaft of the penis

The technique that the woman uses will determine how much of the penis she will take in her mouth. Cover your teeth with your lips and then move in an up and down motion. Apply pulsating pressure with the hand or use a sucking motion on the head of the penis. Using this technique puts you in control and gives you versatility. This also enables you to apply a gentle pressure and twist back and forth, which gives additional sensation and warmth to the shaft of the penis.

Using this technique also gives you an additional hand free. If you so desire you can caress the inside of his thighs with a firm pressure or a gentle scratching motion. Many men enjoy having their testicles fondled while receiving oral sex. As always, be mindful of signals from your lover as to what excites and pleases him. Ask him to guide your hand to the most sensuous part that he likes to have touched.

Finally, using the hand along with your mouth in oral sex gives you versatility. Once you have stimulated the man and gotten to the point where you can feel that he is going to climax and ejaculate, you can (if you want), remove your mouth and continue stimulating the penis with your hand. Or take and move your mouth to the side and just have the penis against your cheek and the sensation and pleasure will continue because you've kept in contact. When you become very intimate like this you will see how honesty in a relationship can enhance the enjoyment of the sexual encounters. Both parties will feel comfortable and confident and be able to show their lovers the parts, positions and type of touch that gives them the most pleasure.

When a women performs oral sex the amount of pressure and suction she puts on is determined by how far the penis is inserted in her mouth. Usually you only want to encompass the head because it gives you more motion and it allows your tongue to create the sucking motion. In addition the amount of suction you can create is better because you have full use of the walls of your mouth and your tongue. Look to your lover and his gestures as to what is the best amount of sucking in order to create desired sensation. This also allows you to use your lips and tongue more effectively. The tongue and lips are very sensuous, and all parts of the body are receptive to their touch. You can use the tongue in different motions inside your mouth and along the penis, creating different feelings of warmth and moisture. If you use your tongue and flick it on the head of the penis in a fluttering butterfly wing motion, it can cause extreme sensitivity and excitement. It is the same type of motion that a man uses when he is stimulating the nipples on a woman. The lighter the touch, the more sensitive and exciting the sensation. One of the most stimulating oral sex techniques doesn't require the woman to have the penis in her mouth, but to use her tongue along the base and shaft of the foreskin of the penis. When properly done, this can cause a mind-blowing sexual experience and climax for the man.

Tea Bagging

This is a term you're starting to hear more and more about. What basically is involved is the woman sucks on a man's balls, either one at a time or both if she's able to handle it. The woman should lay flat on the bed and then have the man crawl over her. When he is in the proper position, you should guide him with your hands by placing them on his waist or his hips and when he's in the proper position she will dip his ball into her mouth. From the same position, as you can imagine, the man will be stimulated and have an erection. You can then incorporate a number of the other techniques or use your tongue and lips to stimulate the shaft of his penis. Remember that the underside of the penis, especially near the frenulum is very sensitive. Using your tongue to stroke or feather the penis will cause a stimulating sensation. Usually most women work on one testicle or ball at a time, but there are lots of techniques that you can apply while in this position.

Cardinal Rule

> When having oral sex with your lover, try to occasionally make some eye contact and see from their gesture and their looks the pleasure that you are providing them with. It is also a guide when you see the facial expressions and gestures when you have hit the right "hot" spots. This will also give you a big ego lift, because you are the one responsible for creating this pleasure.

The Turn-On

Women, if you really want to tease your man, excite him beyond belief and drive him up the wall with a real turn-on all at the same time while making safe sex a fun and exciting thing. Just tell him that the only way

158 • Love, Sex, and Relationships

you know how to put a condom on is with your mouth and lips and say nothing more.

This is a real turn-on for a guy. The thoughts that can run through a man's mind are exciting while at the same time it starts to make the adrenaline pump. No man's going to miss the opportunity to have something exotic done to him like that. So if you have a partner who is nervous or reluctant about using condoms and safe sex, this is a way to overcome that barrier and make it a pleasant and exciting situation.

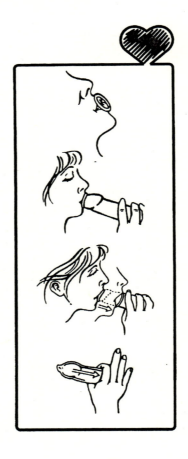

In order to perform this technique you need certain materials and you need to relax and go slowly the first time and have a spare condom handy in case it tears or rips on you.

- **Step 1**: Put your mouth in a kissing position, like a fish kiss. Make sure that your lips are covering your teeth while your mouth is open.
- **Step 2**: Using one of the water based lubricants lube your lips, much like putting on lipstick.
- **Step 3**: Remove from the package the condom and place it in the position so that the reservoir, or nipple, is between your thumb and forefinger. The reservoir, or tip, must be on the bottom. At this time if you're concerned you should put a drop of spermicide on the inside of the condom. Remember the spermicide is for protection against pregnancy and for some STDs. Spermicides aren't harmful, but they don't taste very good, so you do not want to get them on your lips or in your mouth.
- **Step 4**: Now that you have your lips lubricated and you have spermicide inside the condom invert the condom and make sure that the reservoir, or tip is inserted in your lips first so that the unrolled portion of the condom will be in position to roll down over the penis. Another purpose of the spermicide and lubricant is so that it will give a smooth gentle motion while you're unrolling the condom and later greater sensitivity during sexual intercourse.
- **Step 5**: Place the condom in your lips. You may need a slight sucking motion to hold it in place. Make sure that the tip is inserted first, so that the edge as it unrolls will go over the top and slide down over the penis.
- **Step 6**: The penis must be semi-erect or erect for you to do this. Take the penis with one of your hands, place the condom on the tip or head of the penis and make sure that the lubricant does not slip out

too much because it becomes messy and could prevent the condom from staying in place. Now slowly start to push with your tongue gently the condom onto the head of the penis. Try to make sure that you do not trap any air bubbles on the inside of the condom.

- **Step 7:** With you lips over your teeth gently push in a firm slow motion over the rim of the penis and unravel the condom as far down the shaft as is comfortable for you. Remember this will only work if you're using your mouth and your lips, not your teeth. It is also a warm, sensuous feeling that the man receives, because of the combination of your lips, tongue and lubricant. Once you've reached the point where you can't push the condom any further with your lips, then take your fingers and continue to unroll the rest of the condom. Use the fingers to slide the condom the rest of the way to the base of the penis with your thumb and index finger. You must push the condom all the way to the base of the penis, so it will stay in place and offer the proper protection.

If properly done, it should avoid you coming in direct contact with the penis. You will always have the latex barrier between your mouth and the penis. If it makes you nervous and you want to practice, you can practice the same technique with the same steps on a small cucumber, which should work efficiently. If you happen to tear the condom while applying this technique, then take a tissue, remove the condom and lubricant with the tissue, discard in a safe place and start over again with a new condom. Under no circumstances ever use a condom that's been torn or ripped. That's why it is important to make sure that you use your lips and mouth and not your teeth in this technique. A torn condom defeats the purpose of even using a condom.

If both partners are honest and intimate, and have had medical exams, and know that they are free from any sexually transmitted disease and

AIDS, then they can partake in the enjoyment, stimulation and excitement of oral sex without any reservations or doubts. The vagina is a self-cleaning organ and there are no harmful bacteria found in the vagina of a healthy woman. Normal semen is sterile and free from any bacteria. However if you are involved with someone where there is not absolute assurance that they are free from any transmittable disease, then you should use a latex barrier. There are a variety of lubricants on the market today that have been prepared with a flavor, like chocolate, strawberry or banana, which can even make things more interesting and exciting. In the case of a woman, if you are not sure, you need to use a latex barrier. They sell these items at most drugstores. However if it were not readily available, the ideal solution would be to take a latex condom and snip off the tip, and cut it open on one side. I would then recommend that you use one of the monoxial #9 spermicide on the side of the condom that is against the woman. This will also help sensitivity and if you wish you can use one of the flavored lubricants on the side where your lips and tongue will be. In performing cunnilingus on the woman it is recommended that you hold this latex barrier over the entire opening of the clitoris and vagina, you will need to do this probably using both hands. Even though this is somewhat cumbersome, it is still better than contracting an STD.

Performing oral sex or cunnilingus on a woman requires knowledge, sensitivity and practice on the man's part. However the quick rewards for the woman are obvious and the long-term rewards for the man are great.

Techniques That Turn Women On

There are a variety of sensational spots for a man to stimulate with his lips and tongue. The first is the large lips or labia majora. At the tip of the large lips or near the entrance is the hood and the clitoris. This is usually the greatest hot spot for a woman. The tender pinkish skin along the inner side of the vagina opening are the smaller lips, or labia minora, and further in is the vagina. The first inch and half to two inches of the vagina's walls are loaded with nerve endings and are very sensitive. The vagina and the clitoris, like the man's penis, will have a tendency to swell when stimulated, which causes even greater sensitivity.

Gently nudge your lips or tongue against a woman's large outer lips, pushing towards the clitoris underneath. You then have to proceed according to the tenderness and rhythm that the individual woman would prefer. Some like it gentle with a fluttering of the tongue, some like it hard with pressure and rhythm. The best thing is to take a cue from her responses or her instructions. Most of this will rely upon the man's instinct or the guidance from the woman. The amount of pleasure she receives can be heightened or increased along with the other techniques we've discussed regarding the touch and the caress. For example, you could stimulate the nipples and the breast or the inner thighs while at the same time concentrating on the oral stimulation of the clitoris. These techniques will have a tendency to make your sexual encounter not only memorable, but create a unique bond, where one's desires and caring for the other expand and form such a relationship and attachment that sometimes it is difficult to be apart because of the tremendous desire and longing for each other.

Cardinal Rule

> Men should not let intercourse be the only ingredient in a sexual relationship.

What Drives Men Wild

Do you want to make your man your sex slave? Do you want to leave such a powerful impression upon him that he'll beg to see you more and will look forward with anticipation to every time he does? Through this technique you can bind your partner in chains of pleasure. As a woman you be aware of a man's key anatomical points and his greatest areas of sensitivity. This is the head of the penis, or the ring around the penis, which is called the corona. The bottom side of the shaft of the penis, especially near its head, is extremely tender as well. This area is called the frenulum. The ridge of the frenulum is the tissue just under the head of the penis that seems to connect the penis to the shaft. This little area is especially sensitive and should be one of the spots that you concentrate your movement on, because the sensation to your partner is overwhelming.

The first technique we will describe is called "The Slave Maker." This technique, when properly done, can super charge the sexual encounter and can generate an extraordinarily heightened orgasm. The woman should be aware of her man's physical responses, feeling the tension and excitement building in his body and in the shaft of the penis.

In this technique you take the tongue in a very firm motion back and forth along the underside of the penis all the way up to the glans. You create a quick, rhythmic rubbing motion across the head of the penis and that special area just below it. You may wish to have one hand hold the penis in a certain direction, so that it is easier for you to guide your head back and forth. Usually the firmer and quicker the movement, the greater the sensitivity and excitement you will create. This will stimulate the man to a point where, if you continue, he will have a mind blowing sexual climax. Or, once you've got him thoroughly excited and ready, you can then have a joint sexual climax and orgasm together.

What Blows a Man's Mind

The second technique is where the female uses her entire mouth, tongue and lips inserting first the head, then the shaft of the penis into her mouth. In many ways the mouth feels similar to the vagina. Both have qualities of moistness, warmth and softness. However, you can do things with your mouth and tongue that are difficult or impossible to do with your vagina. You can take your tongue and go around and around the rim of the penis, creating sensitivity and excitement. You can use a thrusting motion up and down along the shaft of his penis with your lips, creating a wonderful sensation along his frenulum area. By squeezing your lips against the penis you give another sensation. Sucking on the penis as you would a lollipop can titillate him even further. Be creative and change up or even combine these techniques. Make sure not to forget about your hands, and the pleasure they can provide while your mouth is occupied. As you stimulate the penis you can observe by touch, sight and taste the organ and the sensitivity and size of it as well as the pleasure and satisfaction that it is giving the man.

You can continue this technique until you have obtained such stimulation that the man is ready to have a sexual climax. You can then join him in that, or you can continue and allow him to climax on his own. There are a great number of things that you can add to this form of oral sex. You can use a condom for more than just safe sex and protection. The condom can also be lubricated on the outside with one of the flavored type lubricants or you can buy pre-flavored lubricated condoms. You can also apply chocolate or any one of other items along the head and shaft of the penis and create a kind of joyful and tantalizing situation by slowly and seductively licking it off.

These techniques can either be used as a form of sexual pleasure in themselves or a prelude to something even more.

Cardinal Rule

A good technique during oral sex is to look up and make eye contact with your lover from time to time. This will excite and relax them and show that you can derive pleasure from the contact and touching.

Chapter XVI

Manual Stimulation

Sexual Fantasies

Statistics from surveys and research projects confirm that variety and change can stimulate a relationship. Variety can prevent a relationship from going sour or becoming boring and routine. It is a good exercise to add both energy and romance to your relationship by allowing your fantasies to be fulfilled through experimentation. One of the factors of why boyfriends and husbands supposedly wander is because they expect to find either better or different sex with another partner. However this is rarely true, but that is what their expectations are. In most cases a man is out looking for something different when he already has his fantasy at home, but does not realize it. So, be honest, be intimate and indulge yourself in your fantasies. Be a little adventurous. Add a little spice to your romance and to your relationship. Here's a technique that you may want to try on your boyfriend or husband to add a little excitement to the relationship. This may be extremely pleasurable also for the women who enjoy having their breasts fondled and touched. We'll call this technique the "Keep Your Man at Home" method.

Manual Stimulation

In this section we will now discuss a great number of techniques for manual stimulation to be used on your man. Using these techniques in your foreplay or in your sexual encounters can dramatically change both your sexual relationship and even your life. Remember, the stronger the bond between you and your mate, the more rewarding your erotic adventures will be.

If you have not done so, you may want to try some of these techniques on your man and put him in a state of shock. He may not have even been aware that these things exist and his admiration and pride for you along with his desire will greatly increase.

Techniques That Drive Men Wild

First, take a generous portion of your favorite lubricant or cream and pour it into your man's hands. Then have him gently lubricate your breasts and massage your nipples while rubbing the lubricant all around your breast area. This will relax both of and start to get the man sexual activated, so that his penis will become semi-erect. Next, have the man sit on either the sofa or the bed and you should then sit on the floor below. That way you are in the proper range of motion and are in a comfortable position. Position yourself so that your breasts are near his testicles and shaft of his penis. You can accomplish this by taking your breasts, one in each hand, and holding them up. The next step is to rub in an upward motion your breast and body against his testicles and shaft in the back of the penis. Move the penis and the testicles between your breasts. Then in a kind of rhythm or rocking motion move the penis and testicles back and forth through your breasts, while continuing to put whatever pressure is comfortable to you on your breast against the penis.

How excited you want your man to get is up to you, and how vigorously you rub the shaft of the penis will determine the degree of excitement you create in him. If you wish you could even follow up by having the man lay back on either the sofa or the bed. Straddle him on top and continue to use your body pressure with your breasts to create a rocking or back and forth or a up and down motion. This can be done to the point where the stimulation and the sensitivity become so great that the man climaxes. This technique will cause a lot of excitement, not only because it is unusual, but also because it allows the man to view in close proximity the breasts stimulating the penis. This causes an unusual amount of excitement and stimulation and creates even more anticipation of what is yet to come or what can be done.

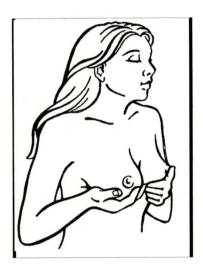
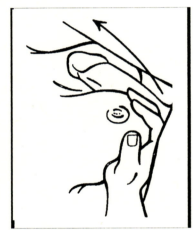

Before you try any one of the following techniques make sure you have some of your favorite lubricants handy. In this case when you're doing manual stimulation, you can even use some of the lubricants we discussed that create the heat and tingling feelings. This can add an extra level of sensation. Position yourself so that you're comfortable, not in an awkward position that will become difficult for you to maneuver in. The enjoyment and fun of these techniques is that they can be performed almost anywhere, so there are a variety of different positions. You can have the man sit on a staircase while you sit on a lower step, on a sofa while you sit on the floor, etc. No matter what position is picked, make sure that you are either sitting or kneeling between his legs in front of him at a lower level. This gives you plenty of area for mobility and comfort and you'll be able to see everything, as will he.

It is usually recommended that you warm the lubricant in your hands before applying it to your man. Remember, you're dealing with an area of his anatomy that can cause him either tremendous pleasure or terrible pain. Although the penis can become very hard when it is erect, the skin is still quite sensitive and that is why we recommend lots of lubricant. It increases the sensitivity and sensation without rawness or irritation.

Try to do all of these techniques in a romantic, seductive way. This will add an extra air of intrigue and excitement for both of you and make the event even more memorable in the man's mind. One final thing, before performing these techniques it is recommended that you remove all jewelry and rings from your hands, especially all of those that might have uneven or ragged edges and be careful with your nails. Used carelessly, long nails can cause excruciating pain.

Since everyone is looking for more variety, we are going to discuss a variety of techniques. However, the positioning and lubricant are common to all.

Womb Technique

This method is usually best done when the women is kneeling in front of the man between his legs while he is in the sitting position. This technique takes a little practice, but once you've done it, it will be comfortable and feel natural. Furthermore, it will definitely impress your man.

- **Step 1:** Take one hand and place it in front of you, fingers up, palm facing away from you.
- **Step 2:** Place your other hand horizontally in front of you and put it palm first at a 90 degree angle against your other hand.
- **Step 3:** Interlock your thumbs, thus creating a cup, or pouch.
- **Step 4:** By gripping your fingers around your vertical hand you will create this pouch or tube effect.
- **Step 5:** Keep your hands relaxed, with the fingers of your vertical hand straight or flexed slightly back. The palm on your vertical hand should be well lubricated. This is the area that will come in contact with the shaft of the penis and create the impression that the penis is entering the vagina. Make sure that your vertical fingers flex back and that your second hand now makes sure that your vertical fingers are forward and at a 90 degree or perpendicular angle to your other hand. Notice from the illustration how the shaft of the penis will move up against the fingers and the palm.
- **Step 6:** With your hands in the position shown, you will take and lower this pouch or tube over the penis. Apply gentle but firm pressure as you stroke. Go slowly at first until you become comfortable with it. What you're going to do is create the sensation of a man penetrating your vagina, so you want to give both the same kind of effect as well as rhythm.
- **Step 7:** Start with a short, slow, up and down motion or rhythm, making sure that the vertical ridge of the hand moves on and over the shaft of his penis and the head. These are the two most sensitive parts of the penis. Also, move your hand so that the web of skin between your thumb and index finger of your horizontal hand is rubbing against the edge of the head of the penis as you move back and forth. This will create additional stimulation and sensation to the penis.

- **Step 8:** Try to develop some form of rhythm or consistency with your strokes and allow as much rubbing at the tip of his penis and along the underlying shaft as you can. If you need to, vary the rhythm, pressure, or length of the strokes. Make sure that your hands are well lubricated, you do not want cause a skin irritation. At the same time, be mindful that the amount of pressure that you apply doesn't end up numbing your lover's penis.
- **Step 9:** Move up and down the shaft of the penis all the way to the base and make sure that your middle finger and index of your vertical hand form into a "V" (as the illustration shows), allowing the penis to go between them. Keep the pressure and rhythm that is most desirable and if you have to make adjustments because of the length of your fingers and nails, do so and do not worry about it. The motion will still cause the sensation you want to develop.
- **Step 10:** Once you have moved your hand down to the base, reverse the downward stroke by dropping the "V" of your vertical hand so that the index and second fingers are now pointing down. Then move your hand back up towards the head of the penis and continue with the steps one through seven over and over again.

Two Hand Job vs. One Hand Job

With both your hands lubricated this is perhaps the easiest of the two hand techniques, however, this can create one hell of a sensation and impression upon your man.

- **Step 1:** Put your hands around the shaft of the penis, one on top of the other, as if you were going to hold a bat. Keep your hands in a closed, firm grip, your thumbs facing you. The grip must be loose enough that you can twist your hands, because they will be moving in opposite directions.

- **Step 2:** In an upward motion you will twist your hands in opposite directions so that the top hand will cover the head of the penis and your thumbs on the top hand will go from facing you to parallel to your left shoulder and the other thumb will be parallel to your right shoulder.
- **Step 3:** In a downward motion reverse the twisting action that you had on the upstroke. Return your hands to your initial position with the thumbs facing you. Your bottom hand will be resting against the man's body at this point.
- **Step 4:** Develop both a rhythm and pressure that is stimulating and pleasing to your man and continue according to his sighs, moans or instructions. This maneuver can be used until he reaches a full climax and orgasm.

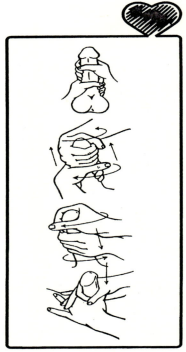

One Hand Job

This technique is so easy and simple you can apply it almost anywhere, even unnoticed. It is virtually the same as the two-hand job above, except using only the one hand—your favorite hand. Develop a sufficient pressure and rhythm to stimulate the penis' head, ring and shaft. Pay special attention to the part connecting the shaft to the head.

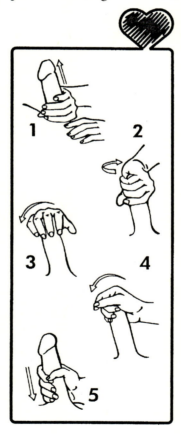

The Gentle Tickle Technique

This technique can be applied from almost any position. It is especially good if you are just starting foreplay and the male has a soft or semi-erect penis. It's also versatile. Once the penis becomes erect you can continue stimulating him while he is stimulating you very easily. Fondle or tickle the head of the penis and the rim. Stroke the area where the foreskin comes together by the rim or head of the penis. As you know, this is a highly sensitive area. After you've done it once or twice you will find out how quickly you can get your man excited. This is also the type of technique that you can do on the sly. Try it under the table in a private place and get him excited as to what is going to happen later. Also for this technique you really don't need lubricant, so it makes it both easy and convenient.

Pile Driver

A number of women have told me that this technique will make your man go wild and it will be memorable. He will remember this, then you can tease or tantalize him later with either a gesture or comment and you can get him excited all over again.

- **Step 1:** Put your hands out in front of you, hanging down. You want to be able to turn your wrist in a twisting motion. It is this action that creates part of the sensation. Your thumbs are held against your index fingers and your palms are facing away from you. Gently start with one hand and hold the base of the penis firmly. You should now be looking at the back of your hand and he should be seeing you thumb. Position your other hand so it will be ready to move into position once the first hand stroke is complete. Once you've developed a rhythm both hands will be in constant motion.

- **Step 2:** Stroke the penis shaft up and down in a continuous motion while maintaining the placement of your hand.
- **Step 3:** On the upstroke when you reach the head, twist your hand as if you were opening a jar. During the whole time, you twist and rub against the top of the penis. This is what causes the stimulation.
- **Step 4:** Try to keep your hands in motion and in contact with the penis at all times. Rotate your hands over the top of the penis as if you were polishing a knob in a slight rubbing or vibrating motion. You will be twisting your hands as a result. The thumb will now be facing you and the back of your hand will be facing him. When you reach the top of the penis and you've come down on the shaft again you will give the knob polish on top and come down firmly to the starting position.
- **Step 5:** At this time you will take your second hand and move it into the new starting position on top of your finishing hand. You want to develop some form of rhythm so that you will be continuously moving both hands and this will develop the sensation. The speed and the pressure will be left up to you and to the signals he is giving you, either through talking to you, or through sighs or gestures. If you start and stop you will lessen the sensation, so you will want to practice. It will become an easy, flowing motion.
- **Step 6:** Once you've developed the motion and rhythm you will alternate with your hands through the preceding steps until he either reaches ecstasy or begs for mercy.

There are variations to this one. You can work on the top of the penis in doing the twisting and rubbing motion around the head. That is more desirable. Or if it is more comfortable for you, you can develop a rhythm using one hand. On the upward stroke, twist and polish the top of the penis and come down on the backward side of the penis. Then continually repeat the motion.

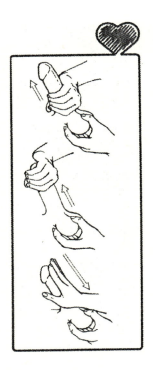

The Grip

- **Step 1:** This technique is similar to the motion that men use on themselves when they are masturbating. After you've lubricated your hands and rubbed them gently to warm them, grasp the base of the penis as if you were grabbing a bat. Your thumb and fingers should come together around the base and you will be looking at the back of your hand.
- **Step 2:** Creating both warmth and pressure your hand will be around the penis.
- **Step 3:** In an even stroke, glide you hand from the base towards the head of the penis, moving your hand to the top of the shaft. However, do not go over the head of the penis. At all times keep

your fingers and hand in contact with the penis. When you reach the top of the penis, pull your hand, palm down along the shaft. It is the same motion that create the stimuli in several of the other techniques. The greatest sensation comes when you rub along the base of the penis and around the crown of the head. You have to, in all of these techniques, develop some sort of rhythm and keep the stimulation constant.

- **Step 4:** Once you've developed motion and rhythm with one hand, your other hand can be massage his testicles. It is a pleasing sensation to many men to have their testicles softly massaged and rubbed.
- **Step 5:** As with any of these techniques you can explore different areas of the body to see what is the most sensitive to your mate. Ask them to guide your hand or tell you where the sensation is the greatest. They will usually respond with some sighs or moans when you've developed a technique that creates a great deal of sensation for them.

Swivel Top

This technique is usually done on a semi or fully erect penis. It's appealing for men who enjoy a firm grip on their penis.

- **Step 1:** Using your one hand, encircle the shaft of the penis with your index finger and thumb. Have a grip much like you would if you had to hold his penis erect. While holding the penis in this position, you can apply some pressure gently. Lightly feel the testicles and almost hold one side. However you do not want to squeeze the testicles directly. This can be very painful and create a lot of discomfort. You want to gently massage the testicle. Once you have a firm grip on the base of the penis then you can go to Step 2.

- **Step 2:** Using your free hand, cup your palm as if you were going to polish a knob and put it on top of the head of the penis. The next step is to twist and rub your hand against the head of the penis as if you were polishing a knob. Slide your hand down the shaft of the penis in a gentle twisting motion, then proceed back to the top. Repeat this movement. The motion is the same as what is detailed in the technique known as the Pile Driver. As in all the techniques, look to your partner's gestures and comments to see what speed of rhythm you should have and what pressure to apply.

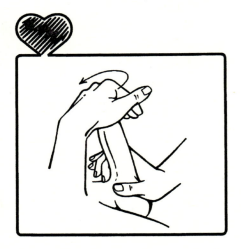

Firemen's Pull

This technique requires that the penis be either semi-erect or erect. All the techniques require that you generously lubricate both of your hands before starting.

- **Step 1:** Put your hands together, interlocking the fingers.

- **Step 2:** Move your thumbs backwards to make a tube or a hole between your palms.
- **Step 3:** Gently slide the opening between your palms over the penis. Make the fit comfortable but firm. In an up and down motion, twisting to the left and then to the right, move up and down the shaft of the penis, stimulating the shaft to the top where it connects to the head of the penis. You'll be able to tell by your partner's sighs or gestures if you should apply more pressure or not.
- **Step 4:** Continue this motion up and down with a rhythm and a constant twisting back and forth. This technique can be used to both stimulate and heighten the excitement or to bring your partner to a complete orgasmic climax.

Firemen's Pull Pump

This technique is basically an expanded version of the Fireman's Pull. To perform this technique, go through all the steps of the Fireman's Pull first.

- **Step 1:** Contract then release your clasped fingers alternately to create a pulsing sensation. The goal is to imitate the vaginal contractions that the penis normally feels during intercourse.
- **Step 2:** It's too awkward to create a pulsing or a squeezing motion as you are going up and down and twisting, just simply stroke up and down while your fingers come together in a clasping, pulsating grip. Keep in mind that you can adjust both the stroke and the pressure of the pulse to suit your man's desires. All of these techniques, as usual, can be used to both stimulate and increase the sensitivity prior to intercourse or to bring to a full sexual climax and orgasm. Use a generous amount of lubricant.

Guiding

We have discussed at length that it creates a desirable relationship when both people can be honest and intimate. This technique is an opportunity to get a feel and impression for each other while at the same time showing your partner what provides you with the greatest amount of pleasure. Sometimes it is difficult for people to discuss or to verbally express their sexual desires, but this technique is great for getting involved in a very intimate way. Both you and your lover should generously lubricate your hands and slightly warm the palms. You can even lightly blow on the palms. This in and of itself can be quite sensuous.

- **Step 1:** Place your hands on either side of his erect penis. The bottom of your hands should be resting on his stomach with your palms facing each other, the penis being held in between.
- **Step 2:** Have your partner place his hands on the outside of yours and ask him to guide the motion of your hands. You can see from how he holds your hands and guides them what type of motion and rhythm he prefers.
- **Step 3:** As he's guiding your hands on the up and down stroke, ask him which feels better. Try different techniques or motions. Add a pulsing grip to the shaft of the penis on the down stroke much like you did in the Fireman's Pull/Pump. Take the thumbs and as you come up to the head of the penis run them along the rim and see how that feels. You will find out soon which motion and rhythm creates the greatest stimulation and delight for him and you will get first hand a feeling for the type of pressure and rhythm you should use in the other techniques.

Fourth of July

The motions of this technique are primarily on the shaft of the penis, giving a clear view when the man reaches a sexual climax and has an ejaculation. That's why we call it the 4th of July.

As always, lubricate both of your hands, rub them to warm them and if you wish blow on them.

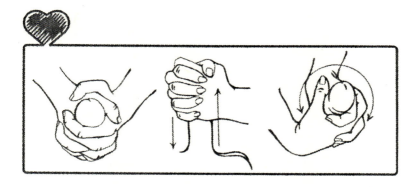

- **Step 1:** With your hands facing the palms, almost in a praying gesture, place the shaft of the penis between your hands resting against the palms. Your hands should be on the base of the shaft against his body. The head of the penis should be above the palms of the hand.
- **Step 2:** Move your hands slowly back and forth, rubbing the shaft of the penis. As the lubricant starts to warm up, increase the motion and speed of the rubbing. The feeling to the penis is that of a twilling motion, like when you spin a stick with your hands. While rubbing, start the up and down strokes along the shaft of the penis, but don't go over the rim of the head.

- **Step 3:** Once you've created a comfortable rhythm or motion, continue with back and forth as well as up and down strokes. Add more lubricant if necessary. Be careful not to rub too hard. This can cause discomfort or even injury.
- **Step 4:** With the same motion you can add different variations or options, depending on how you feel and the sensations you are creating for your partner. For example, you can add a pulsating effect to the rubbing back and forth. You can occasionally change the strokes up and down to clasped hands and then go back to the back and forth rubbing motion as well as the up and down strokes.

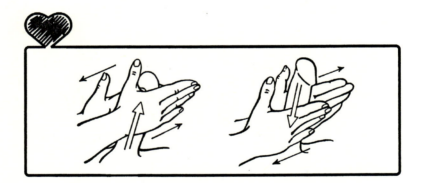

The Virgin

This technique creates a special sensation, because you will give the impression of the penis penetrating the women's vagina all the way down. With the motions and the positions of your hands you will create the feeling that many men enjoy of being deeply inside a woman. This is a very sensuous manual stimulation. It gives an exotic feeling to the man, while at the same time allowing him to view fully your gestures and body. Comments that we have received regarding this technique indicates that not only does it really, really excite the man, but that it is also such a sensuous thing that both the man and the woman become excited and stimulated.

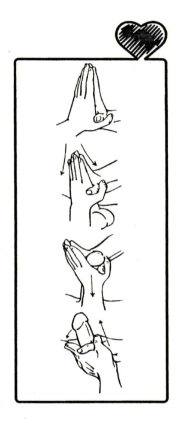
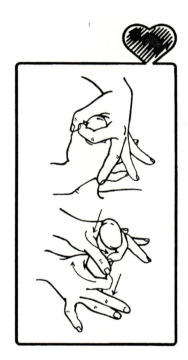

- **Step 1:** Place your hands in front of you palms together, fingers facing upward, with the thumbs interlocked or over lapping. This would resemble almost the typical gesture of praying hands. You will hold your hands breast height.

- **Step 2:** You need to be very close to the man to perform this and you must have enough motion in your forearms and elbows. Your fingers will remain firmly together as well as the thumbs crossed.
- **Step 3:** Slowly lower your hands over the head of the penis, enclosing the it within the hole created by your hands. Keep your fingers together and adjust the pressure so that the penis is firmly in place. Then, using a downward stroke you will feel the motion of the penis head between your palms. Keeping the pressure on, move the strokes up and down along the shaft, making sure that your thumbs are crossed.
- **Step 4:** On the downward stroke when you reach the base of the shaft of the penis your fingers should be pointing up towards his face with your hands together and crossed in front of you. Repeat this up and down stroke with sufficient pressure and if you want to you can add a little bit of a pulse to it at the same time. This one will probably give the closest impression of penetration into a woman. Repeat steps 2 to 4.

The Big OK

- **Step 1:** This one is very easy and quick. Just take both your hands and form the OK sign where the thumb and the forefinger come together.
- **Step 2:** With a firm, but gentle movement, slide the penis through the opening of the OK ring.
- **Step 3:** As you are stroking downward, twist your left hand to the left and your right hand to the right. Once you hit the base with one hand on top of the other, then return with an upstroke, continuing the twist.
- **Step 4:** Once you have established the motion and rhythm, start the left hand going down, while the right hand goes up. Alternate the

up and down strokes and the twisting action so that both hands will meet in the middle of the shaft as one goes towards the top while the other heads for the bottom. Once they hit the top and the bottom, start their movement again back towards the other end. Add sufficient pressure so that it is a firm grip and that it causes a stimulating, tingling sensation. Always look for the reaction of your lover. Pay attention to his sighs, gestures, his guiding hand or his voice commands.

Big Squeeze

- **Step 1:** With both hands well lubricated, take hold firmly of the shaft of the penis with either hand.
- **Step 2:** With your hand cupped as if you're reaching for a round door knob, grasp the head of the penis. Come down as if you were holding an orange and were going to squeeze it on a juicer. The ends of your fingers should flare out around the head of the penis as you come down. This will give a warm, moist sensation to the head.
- **Step 3:** Once you've grabbed the head of the penis gently but firmly move back and forth as if you were twisting a doorknob to open and close.
- **Step 4:** Reverse the movement, but still keep a firm feeling on the penis with your fingers as you move upwards, so that you give the sensation of feathering over the head of the penis. Start your downward stroke again, twisting and squeezing like you're opening a doorknob. Keep repeating this motion and you will create a sensational feeling of excitement and stimulation that can eventual lead to orgasm.

Polish the Knob

The two following techniques should be used while your lover is sitting up on the edge of a bed, sofa, or someplace where you can have freedom of motion and be able to be in front of him. For this technique it is best not to use a lubricant. You will need a piece of very soft material, like satin or velvet.

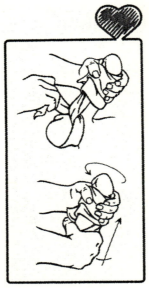

- **Step 1:** With your lover facing you, take one hand and hold the penis up and away from the body.
- **Step 2:** Take the piece of soft cloth and wrap it around the shaft of the penis.
- **Step 3:** With a gentle pull and twisting motion you will begin to work your way up and down the shaft of the penis. Depending on the sensitivity you will apply more or less pressure and move faster or slower until you arrive at the right combination that cause the greatest stimulation and excitement.

- **Step 4:** A variation is you can take the material or fur and cradle his testicles with it, rubbing it against them gently. Some men find this very exhilarating. Or if you wish, you can wrap the material or fur around in a motion where it cradles the testicles and comes up around the shaft of the penis. With a twisting back and forth of the material you will stimulate both the testicles and the shaft at the same time. You can experiment. If you feel that a lubricant will add better motion and more sensitivity, then add some. However usually the softness of the material and how firm you pull the material are the things that determine the feeling and sensation. Velvet and fur seem to create the greatest sensation of all.

Pump and Twist

This technique requires both hands. Make sure that you apply a generous amount of lubricant to both hands. You will need it for this technique.

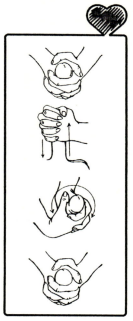

- **Step 1:** Clasp your hands together, interlacing the fingers.
- **Step 2:** Relax your hands and thumbs to make a hole.
- **Step 3:** Clasp both hands together and lower them over his penis. Keep a firm, snug grip. You will give a sensation of both warmth and moisture to the penis.
- **Step 4:** Gently start to move your clasped hands up and down the shaft of the penis.
- **Step 5:** As you do this, add a slight twisting motion. Move your hands up and down gently but firmly, pulsing your hands, contracting the clasped hands. This will take some practice. However, find a rhythm that's good for you and him.
- **Step 6:** Put it all together, moving up and down the shaft while giving a pulse and a twist. If it's too difficult to enter the twisting motion, then just utilize the pulsating grip. This technique will bring him quickly to a sexual climax. If he starts to ejaculate keep the motion going, however soften the grip and do it more gently. This will create even more sensation and give him a real rush. Do not be too firm or too strong at this point, because the man will be very sensitive and it could interrupt his pleasure.

Lasting Impression

Apply a generous amount of lubricant to your hands and rub them together to warm up your hands and lubricant. This is an easy technique and what is nice about it is it can also be incorporated very easily into the oral sex techniques.

- **Step 1:** Take the penis in both hands, almost like you would be holding a baseball bat. With the thumbs facing you. Position the hands so they are comfortable and well lubricated.

- **Step 2:** You will be moving each of the hands in opposite directions, so your hands will twist as you're moving up or down on the penis. At one point your thumbs will be facing you, and the other twisting motion the thumbs will be facing your opposite shoulders.
- **Step 3:** On the down stroke, bring your hands all the way down so your fingers rub against his stomach.
- **Step 4:** Continue this motion up and down until you come to a comfortable, pleasing rhythm. You should be able to tell by his facial signs or sighs the stimulation and pleasure that you're giving him. If you want, at this point you can also massage the head of the penis with your tongue. This increases the sensation and stimulation. Or you can run the rim of the penis with your lips. This will add additional moisture, heat and create a sensation much like that of intercourse. That's why we call this technique "Lasting Impression."

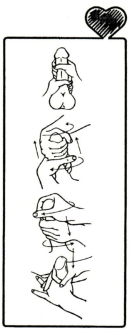

Cardinal Rule

> All the manual stipulations are best when you're using lubricant and your hands are warm and you use enough pressure to create the tingly sensation.

Manual stimulation is a preference of some. Some men actually have a greater sexual climax and orgasm through hand manipulation than through intercourse. It is up to the couples to work together and guide each other regarding motion, rhythm and firmness. If the skin becomes too sensitive it will become irritable and cause discomfort or pain, so be aware that you need to use sufficient lubricant at all times.

If you're going to bring your man to sexual climax and orgasm, it is best to have a towel handy when he ejaculates. If you want to really impress the man and make him feel pampered, you can use the Oriental style. Get a washcloth, put it in hot steaming water, drop a few drops of lemon oil on it, squeeze it out, bring it over and drape it over his penis and his entire groin area and wipe him off. This will create a warm tender feeling that is both soothing and cleansing at the same time. Furthermore, this kind of pampering will make him crazy.

Masturbation

Masturbation is almost always done alone and in most cases is the result of exploring one's own body and creating stimulation that usually ends in a climax and orgasm.

Masturbation helps us understand our own sexuality and pleasure spots. No one teaches us how to masturbate, it is an instinctive behavior caused by our sex drives. Therefore, use this knowledge to show your partner how to enjoy your body and what areas give you the greatest pleasure.

Unfortunately because of many myths in our culture about masturbation, many people feel awkward discussing things they have learned about their bodies. If this is the case, then guide your partner's movements, show them what pleases you. You have the right to enjoy their touch, and enjoy your body.

Exploring Masturbation

Masturbation is natural and fun. It is the exploring time when people can find out about their own body and sense the parts of their body. It gives them the opportunity to release the sexual drives without engaging in sexual intercourse. It allows privacy and gratification, because sexual intercourse and interplay is not always appropriate or possible.

Masturbation usually takes place in the early puberty time of a boy and girl. However it may continue throughout a person lifetime because of the frustration they incur when they have sexual relations with another person and are not receiving sexual gratification or climax.

Sexual stimulation by masturbation produces an orgasm because the stimulation if so great for both the man and the woman. Masturbation may refer to almost any sexual conduct except sexual intercourse.

Masturbation takes place for many reasons. The physical changes in a person's body during puberty usually causes exploration. People then discover the sensitivity and stimulation they have in certain areas. A young boy or girl's first sexual experiences are usually through masturbation. Usually a young boy will grasp his penis after he becomes somewhat aroused and by stroking it repeatedly he will create enough sexual activity and stimuli that he will eventually have a sexual climax and orgasm.

Girls discover how sensitive the clitoris is and how stimulating it is to touch the vagina. Usually they create sexual stimuli by rubbing their clitoris. Many times girls will have objects they lay on or rub against, like a pillow, while they are pushing themselves towards a sexual climax.

There are many cultural and religious taboos against masturbation. Often these different social prohibitions against intercourse and premarital sex put the children in an awkward, anxiety filled situation. A lot of guilt and anxiety can be created when natural drives and curiosity cause children and young adults to become actively involved in masturbating. However, guilt should not be laid on a person, especially in their teen years, for masturbating unless they do it excessively and there are other determining factors.

From all the research and medical reports, there is no evidence that masturbation is harmful in any way. In fact, most medical reports will explain that masturbation is a natural evolution and progression that almost everyone experiences at one point or another in the development of their sexuality.

Male Masturbation

Usually young boys start off masturbating by grabbing their semi erect or erect penis and stroking its shaft or head until they are sexually aroused enough where they have a sexual climax or orgasm. Sometimes they use a lotion or do it while they are bathing with soap, which gives more sensitivity. Another method is pressing the erect penis against a pillow or mattress while thinking sensuous thoughts and moving in an up and down manner.

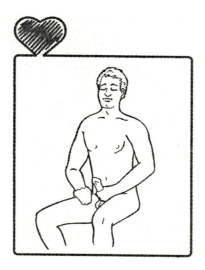

From that point on preference dictates technique. The pattern of male masturbation may carry on throughout one's life depending on a person's sexual activity and anxiety.

Female Masturbation

Most young girls aren't too knowledgeable about the clitoris and its activity and purpose. Usually the clitoris is encountered by accident through self exploration. They will then find that it is a pleasant sensation to rub it and to stimulate it. Eventually through rubbing and massaging the clitoris or the vagina they bring themselves to a sexual climax and orgasm. Similar to men the women may cause stimulation by using a pillow or blanket or other items that they can rub up against while putting pressure on the object. This will stimulate the vagina and sometimes the clitoris if done in the proper motion.

Later in life, many women, including those in active, healthy sexual relationships, find masturbation to be their sole source of sexual gratification. Research and questioning sessions have revealed that many women stimulate themselves prior to or after a sexual encounter to release the pent up sexual energy and to satisfy the sexual drives. Again this reinforces the reason why in a good relationship the foreplay is so important. There are a number of different techniques described within this text that show how to stimulate the woman's clitoris simultaneously while having sexual intercourse with her so that she will be able to heighten her sensitivity and stimulation and reach an orgasm.

It may be difficult for some to realize why young teens will masturbate. Adults feel that adolescents aren't mature enough or ready for a sexual relationship, which is true. However, that does not cover that the primary reason why young people masturbate. They do so because in addition to exploring, they are experiencing a wild new form of stimulation. The sexual climax can be such a physical happening to them that it can almost become addictive. There may not be anything else that they can compare it with. As a result, some young people can become very prone to early or excessive masturbation.

It is important that you note that the need to masturbate shouldn't be confused with the need for relationships and sexual intercourse. That unfortunately is the problem when many do not realize the difference and prematurely become sexually active with the opposite sex. This is not a desirable situation, because as we've explained clearly in the first part of the book, people haven't physically, mentally or emotionally developed sufficiently to fully comprehend and perform in a manner that is necessary to establish a complete and fulfilling sexual relationship. When a person attempts to do this too early in life, many times the emotional scars from the bad experience are long lasting and will cause a major impasse. This may prevent them from developing healthy relationships later on in life.

One final note regarding masturbation: Because the mind is so important in stimulating the sexual glands, some girls are capable of having an orgasm by stimulating and fondling their breasts and nipples. Many women, because of their anatomy, can masturbate by crossing their legs and rubbing their thighs together. This action will in some cases cause the outer lips of the vagina to rub against the clitoris and stimulate it, which will eventually cause enough sexual stimulation for an orgasm. Also, girls may stimulate themselves by inserting objects other than their hands and fingers in the vagina. The variety of objects documented is unbelievable, but this is not a good technique. You should never put a foreign object in your vagina. There is always a chance of abrasions, and bacteria or other foreign matter will most likely make their way in as well. Some of these sex objects and toys are much like the manufacturers who make high fashion shoes. They may think it's practical, but they are not the one who use or wear them. As a result they can cause harm or damage. Thus be careful if you use any type of object to stimulate yourself.

Women, more so than men because of cultural or religious beliefs, often find that their only form of sexual release and enjoyment is through masturbation. Unmarried women especially express that masturbation is part of their regular routine. Many times masturbation is largely exploratory in nature. Women sometimes will try to stimulate themselves with their legs spread apart, criss-crossed or held together. Some women stated that pressing their legs together after climaxing gave them a longer and greater sensitivity that would travel all the way through their thighs and sometimes into their mid section. It also should be noted from the Hite Report that a great many women who experience orgasms with a male during sexual intercourse engage in some form of self stimulation either before, during or after the act. Many times they hide this self gratification from their partners.

Chapter XVII

Secrets to Make Intercourse Fantastic

Lovemaking Every Which Way

Sex is a pleasant experience. It should be pleasurable for you. Keep it that way by following these simple techniques. First off, relax and release all tension and anxiety. Get yourself mentally in the mood. Think about the pleasant and exciting things about being close. Anticipate the touch and sensations. Have intimacy and honesty with your partner. Don't be afraid to experiment with both touching and positions. All lovemaking positions are not the same for everyone. In fact, some positions may be uncomfortable for certain people. For instance, if a man or woman has either back, hip or knee problems, then the different positions will cause undo pain and discomfort and reduce the enjoyment and pleasure you should be getting from both foreplay and sexual intercourse. Be patient. Be sympathetic to the other person's needs and responses. Men, in some cases, must learn to take their time. Enjoy as you're going along. Sometimes the journey or trip can be more pleasurable than the arrival.

The reason this book was written was to remove the one great myth that has been repeated through centuries by our parents, peers, doctors or friends. The myth is that sex is something that "will come naturally to you." The propagation of the species comes naturally, but unfortunately for most developing a good relationship and having explosive, satisfying sex does not come naturally. In fact many men are inept lovers simply because they've had no training in the proper techniques. Because of the veil of secrecy, false myths and rumors have gone on for centuries. These myths will be discussed and revealed to you in this book. Both men and women because of the mass media, romantic novels and our movie industry have been given a false impression of what a sexual relationship should be. Many people have never had the opportunity to fully understand and appreciate what a good sexual relationship is all about. They have been mislead by these forms of media and myths. We have been frustrated, disappointed and many times exasperated. Research has revealed a great number of woman who feel that men are feeble when it comes to really creating the excitement and satisfaction that they are so longing for.

As we have tried to drive home throughout the book, the keys to heightening your sexual relationship are intimacy and honesty. After utilizing the different methods and techniques for increasing or heightening your sexual activity, get feedback from your partner. Once you've done this then it is very easy to have a pleasure rich sexual relationship where both parties can be satisfied, fulfilled and reach the sexual climaxes and orgasms they both desire.

It is not necessary for sexual intercourse to be a male dominant activity. As a matter of fact, by learning new positions and techniques you can make the experience for both more of an **orgasmic pleasure.**

Ready, Set, Live Life to the Fullest

By practicing and incorporating the different techniques regarding kissing, fondling, foreplay and oral or manual stimulation you can bring all the secrets of sexual pleasure into play, so that the sexual intercourse you have with your loved one produces not only a momentary stimulation, but a feeling of satisfaction, pleasantness, fulfillment, love, excitement all while providing orgasms that are beyond belief.

Cardinal Rule

> The benefits of sex are vastly underrated. Good sex is an emotional stimulator. It can produce good morale and build up your ego while providing physical side effects and benefits. The adrenaline that is released during a good sexual encounter has been documented to help people who are suffering from asthma, allergies, anxiety and even arthritis. The physical benefits and sensations that are created at times can not be described. The tremendous exhilaration and release of energy and stimulation is an excellent conditioner for pumping up the heart.

Techniques to Create Orgasms for Women

The research studies have established that the majority of women do not experience a sexual climax and an orgasm during normal intercourse. As a result this can sometimes leave tremendous disappointment, anxiety and guilt on the woman and is what causes many of them to "fake" an orgasm. Actually as few as 30% of women reach climax during intercourse. Therefore, we will start off with the different positions and techniques that will almost ensure that your woman has a climax during intercourse. We want to heighten the sensitivity and intimacy by being able to orgasm while in the act of intercourse. In this way, neither the man or woman will experience disappointment. Both can let go of their worries and enjoy the wonderful sensations generated by the pleasant stimulation of their genital areas.

This is as beneficial to the woman as it is to the man, because men's egos are deflated when they think that the woman hasn't been sexually fulfilled. Conversely, men's egos can almost burst if they think they are creating a tremendous sensation and the woman is going wild.

The reason I put extra emphasis on this section is that throughout the centuries so much has been talked about and discussed about how to excite and arouse a man when, fortunately for men by nature, they are very easy to arouse. Any normal healthy man can usually become sexually aroused very easily. As we have discussed in the prior sections, the vast majority of men, once becoming aroused and stimulated, will have a climax during intercourse. They usually receive sufficient stimulation for this. For centuries women have been faking orgasms or have been in a sort of sexual cocoon, not realizing what a true orgasm was and what they were missing out on. As a result, this fact has caused many false myths. Over the years it's been a mystery to men why women were not enjoying or participating in sex to the extent that men would like to at times. The real reason is that women had become exasperated, frustrated and bored, because in many situations the sexual pleasure was all one sided. The man was the receiver and the woman was the giver.

For the sexual bond to remain strong, the relationship needs to be equal and enjoyable for both partners every time they come together. In this way people create strong emotional and sexual bonds. A woman will not need another man, and a man will not need another woman, because they have each been fulfilled and satisfied.

The key to having satisfying, rewarding, exciting, super-charged intercourse is proper stimulation, starting with kissing, touching, stroking and manual stimulation. It is essential for the man to remain aware of his woman's "hot spots," such as her "G" spot, clitoris, large lips, nipples and vagina. This not only is pleasurable in and of itself, but it also has multiple rewards for both parties and sets the proper stage for reaching a climax and orgasm during intercourse.

Remember we said earlier that women are more than capable of multiple orgasms in a relatively short time. Nothing can create a longer lasting, better impression on a woman than if a man can satisfy her in such a way as to stimulate her multiple times during their sexual encounter.

If your woman becomes stimulated to the point that she has a sexual climax and orgasm during your foreplay, this is excellent. Merely continue the very gentle like manner of stroking or stimulation and make sure that the clitoris has been properly stimulated and massaged. It is recommended that you use a lubricant because the clitoris is very sensitive and may become raw before penetration. This is one way of ensuring that during intercourse the woman will have enough stimulation and sensation herself to fully enjoy the sex and at the same time experience an orgasm.

Sure—Fire

Some women have said that this is a sure fire way to stimulate the clitoris in order to have a sexual climax and reach an orgasm while they are having intercourse with a man. The technique involves sexually arousing and stimulating the woman by a sensuous teasing with a soft gentle stimulation of the clitoris.

As we've discussed in the section *THE MAGIC OF TOUCH*, start off using your hands and fingers, gently caressing the different sensitive parts of the woman while embracing and sensuously kissing her. Use the light scratching caress we've discussed and trace your fingers along the most responsive parts of her body. Pay special attention to the area around the breasts. However, make sure your grip isn't too strong or vigorous. The goal is to make love to the woman, not attack her. Overly aggressive fondling turns off most women, and rightfully so.

You want to softly caress your partner. Play lovingly with her breasts, abdomen and inner thighs. Maintain an almost teasing manner. Don't charge towards her vagina, or even her nipples. Let anticipation build up. Let the woman relax and enjoy the touching, whetting her appetite for more. This foreplay will give the man ample opportunity to become both emotionally and physically aroused. At this point, it will be the man's natural instinct to rush into intercourse. However, patience can be well rewarded. The intelligent male will wait until the woman is as aroused as he is, or even more so. Then she will beg for release and won't be shy of communicating about how to go about doing it.

At this point you will continue stimulating and teasing her by taking your penis and gently rubbing it against her clitoris. Allow her to help with the rhythm and the firmness.

Slowly and gently go a half inch back and forth around the inner lips of the vagina, never truly penetrating, while at the same time rubbing the head of the penis against the clitoris. The initial contact of penetration pleasures a woman's most sensitive areas, namely the lips of her vagina and her clitoris. The more you tease, rub or caress this area, the more she can become aroused. A woman can become so emotionally turned on that the teasing will start to drive her wild. Eventually she will crave full penetration and the final stimulation of the clitoris. At this point, one sexual climax can be just the start of things. Women respond very quickly and are quite capable of having multiple orgasms. It is like a double header and extremely exciting for the woman. This can also be very gratifying to the man, because he receives a tremendous boost to his ego as well as experiencing a tremendous sexual explosion when he has his orgasm. There is nothing more exhilarating than when both bodies have been teased to such an extent that neither one can stand it any longer and they totally give in to each other and experience at the same time the ecstasy of orgasm.

When people experience together a fulfilling and satisfying sexual relationship this creates not only anticipation and longing, but a lasting bond that helps strengthen and bring together the total relationship.

Finally, if the women who have discussed this with me are correct, the sexually explosive orgasm that you will experience from this technique will leave an everlasting impression and desire within you.

In some cases the woman may need additional stimulation while having intercourse. There are three distinct positions that you can have sexual intercourse in while continuing to stimulate the woman's clitoris with your hands.

In spite of all the movies you've seen and stories you've read, the traditional man on top position (the missionary position) is probably the least desirable one for intercourse. We'll explain more later. The position that stimulates the female the most during sex is the woman on top or the female superior position. This position affords many benefits for both the man and woman. The man can stimulate the clitoris with his thumb or fingers until the woman desperately wants to climax and orgasm. This position allows for deeper penetration. It allows the woman to help with the thrusting and rhythm, thus giving her more stimulation and enjoyment. It is more compatible if either the woman or the man is much taller than their partner. For the man it has many benefits, not the least of which is the freeing up of his hands. He can look at the woman, admiring her body while massaging her breasts.

The second position is the side-by-side position. This position increases the chances that the woman will be stimulated sufficiently so that she can orgasm the same time the man does. This also enables the man to reach over with his hand and stimulate the clitoris with his thumbs or fingers.

The third position is for the man to enter from behind, where the woman is virtually sitting on top of him. This allows him the opportunity to reach around in front and to stimulate the clitoris and vagina with his hands.

These three essential positions allow the woman to participate along with the man in stimulating the clitoris and vagina. In each of these motions the woman can put sufficient pressure on the pelvic bone area and can position herself so that her clitoris receives exactly the kind of stimulation she wants. She can help control and set both the motion and pressure of the thrusting and help create the proper rhythm. It is these three positions that are most often used to properly stimulate and generate a sexual climax in a woman. The woman is also more directly in control of where the thrust of the penis goes, so she feels the sensation of it hitting the right location for the "G" spot. She can help continue and direct the thrusting. Also women should exercise and try to gain enough muscle control to deliberately create the pulsating effect. This is both a stimulant to the woman and to the man that enhances and increases the sensitivity and enjoyment of the sexual encounter. At the very end of the final chapter there is a brief outline on some techniques that women can use to exercise and increase their muscular control.

You should realize by this time that the power and capability are within your hands to increase and heighten the enjoyment, satisfaction, and excitement that you receive from a fulfilling sexual relationship. The rewards are ten-fold compared to the effort that you will put in. The means are within your grasp and when we discuss the benefits of the different positions of sexual intercourse you will be able to imagine in your mind's eye the benefits each have in addition to the foreplay that can be involved with each of these positions. One final word before we start, remember the step about safe sex. Never become too excited. Always engage in safe sex. Make sure that you have a latex condom, spermicide, lubricant, latex gloves and a box of tissues. Having these items handy should be taken as a sign of class. It shows that you care for both yourself and your lover. Furthermore, what you're doing will enhance your sexual experience, generating pure excitement and enjoyment without any regret.

When you stimulate both the clitoris and the vagina, expect the woman to ejaculate during her orgasm just as a man does. It's convenient to have a box of tissues, a towel or a warm, moist washcloth handy. Both the semen from the man and the fluid from the woman are virtually bacteria free and are not harmful if both the man and woman are free from any sexually transmitted diseases. Still, if you're not in a monogamous relationship, take the precaution of using a condom or latex glove with proper spermicides and lubricants. When discarding the items be of utmost care that the fluids do not come in contact with your skin, especially if you have any open cuts or abrasions.

Be conscientious with your partner and always plan ahead.

Never hesitate to counter any vaginal dryness with a lubricant. This not only increases the sensitivity, but it also prevents any chaffing or soreness to the vagina or the penis. When you're using a condom, be mindful to prevent any breakage or tears in the condom.

The stubble from a shaved pubic region can damage a condom in certain cases. If you do have any rough stubble, take some protective action and use extra lubricant.

The Positions of Lovemaking

Your fantasies, desires and preferences will ultimately determine which position or positions are most satisfying for you and your partner in lovemaking. Trying new positions not only adds spice to your relationship, but it can also increase your desire to be close together more often.

The Missionary Position

The so called missionary position is probably the most commonly used position that you see in books and movies. It is typically thought of as the Western cultural position. In this position the lovers are face to face, with the man on top of the woman. Some believe it's the only correct position, even though many case studies show that this position most often does not satisfy the woman.

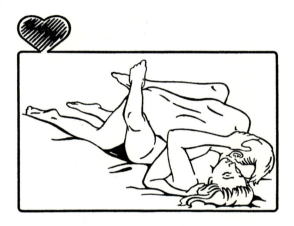

This position can cause problems, especially for the male. This is because he's supporting his weight with his shoulders and his weakest back muscles. He has to use his hands to support himself and therefore he cannot touch or caress the woman, let alone stimulate her clitoris directly.

From the woman's viewpoint, the missionary position has a disadvantage. In many cases during penetration the clitoris is only indirectly stimulated by the penis. In certain women, it is not stimulated at all and therefore it is very difficult for the woman to reach an orgasm. Research has shown that sometimes women don't realize what they are missing. Many aren't aware that they haven't been properly stimulated until they are finally excited by a different position, technique or lover.

Often the missionary position isn't beneficial for the man because he is supporting his weight with his hands and he has a tendency to rush. He goes with vigorous, deep thrusting motions even though the greatest stimulation for both is along the head of the penis and on the inner lips of the woman. Also, this quick deep thrusting may induce the man to have a premature ejaculation and reach climax before either of them are completely satisfied.

If your lover believes that quick, deep, thrusting gives you enjoyment, then slow him down and show him how much greater the enjoyment is for you both. Control him if you have to with your thighs. When you squeeze your thighs around his body, you slow him down and also control how much of his penis you allow inside you. This way you control both the stimulation you receive and the speed. The man will last longer and you can become more aroused. He will soon learn how to do it on his own, once he realizes how much it pleasures you both. His ego will be rewarded especially when you reach a juicy, delicious sexual climax.

The man does not have the freedom to use his hands while in the missionary position and thus cannot touch or stimulate the woman. However, some women prefer this position because it allows the man to kiss the woman and it makes them feel more romantic.

If the woman is not getting any enjoyment or satisfaction from the missionary position, then I recommend that you try the coital alignment technique. Instead of penetrating the woman straight on, which is usually done in the missionary position, the man will ride high so that his pubic bone (the portion of surface just above the shaft of the penis) is applying pressure directly to her mons area (the are of the vagina beneath which the clitoris lies). By using a gentle rhythm, the man will move or rock his pubic bone back and forth over her clitoris, instead of penetrating in a thrusting in and out or quick jerky fashion. This technique will usually stimulate the woman where it is needed.

After using this technique several times, the woman should experience more excitement and enjoyment. She will probably reach an orgasm and climax either during the action or simultaneously with her partner.

The woman can assist in making sure that during penetration she puts pressure on her clitoris. As the man rocks or bears down, the woman can apply counter pressure by pushing up with her pelvis. It would also be helpful if both of them got into a sexual rhythm or pace in order to give a gentle but firm stimulation to each other. The woman should remember to be comfortable bending her knees and resting her legs either on the man's thighs or wrapping them around his neck. However, if she makes herself immobile, she will not be able to get into a rhythm with her pelvis and will defeat the action the man is taking because she will not be properly stimulated. At the same time, the man should rest his weight on the woman and bear down in a gentle but firm rocking manner.

The woman should woman reach orgasm before the man, because when the man reaches an orgasm it's all over. The penis will become soft and he will not be able to continue to stimulate the woman.

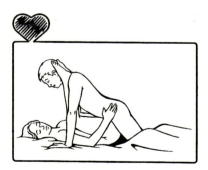

Top Side

Since pleasure and satisfaction are part of the goal of sexual intercourse, the woman on top position is many times mutually satisfying.

The reason for this is that a woman on top is better able to fine tune the stimulation to her clitoris. In this position both partners can mutually enjoy the experience and reach an orgasm and climax. This is also more enjoyable many times for the man because it does not put any undo pressure or strain on his back, arms or shoulders. It allows him to caress the woman, having full use of both hands. He can also find mutually rewarding stimulation from fondling the breasts or stroking other parts of the woman's body. Or, if she requests, the man can stimulate her clitoris. The position of woman on top also has other advantages because both parties have a tendency to last longer and not get as tired since the woman's strongest muscles are supporting her. Both his hands are free to touch and caress her body and this leaves the woman's hands free to caress and help stimulate the man if necessary. The woman can reach back and massage the man's testicles. It has also been learned from interviews that men will have a tendency to last longer when the woman is on top. They are not so prone to early ejaculation and climax. Try to let the woman control how rapidly things proceed to climax. The top side position can be mutually satisfying for both parties.

Back Side

In nature, most primates have sexual intercourse with the man penetrating the female from the back. This rear entry intercourse can seem animalistic, and therefore some people feel uncomfortable using it. On the flip side, it's also the reason why it has a lot of appeal. This position can be done with the woman standing up bent over, on all fours or laying flat.

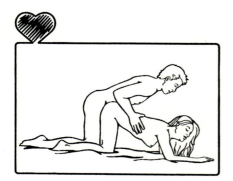 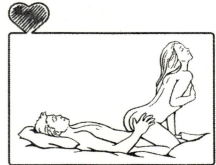

The rear entry position has some major advantages. First, it is probably the position in which the man can penetrate the deepest. Secondly, it is the position with the least amount of stress and discomfort for a woman during late pregnancy. From case studies, women who have a very sensitive G spot located on the front top wall of their vagina report that it is usually stimulated when the man enters her from behind. The disadvantage of rear entry is that the woman's clitoris receives almost no stimulation and therefore she may not experience an orgasm. It may leave her wanting for additional stimulation when the man has completed. It is also sometimes difficult for men to keep their penis inside the vagina in this position. Some men may worry that their partner might think that they are homosexual because they are using this position. However, this is not true and should not discourage you from trying this technique.

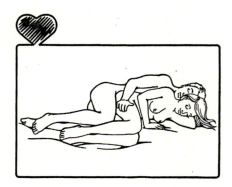

A second rear entry position is where the woman sits on the man. This position allows the woman to set the speed and rhythm and to stimulate herself to reach a full orgasm.

Face to Face on the Side

This method or technique is particularly nice because if your partner is tired, sick, old, or in the late months of pregnancy, it is a gentle position. It helps the man last longer. The partners lie on their side face to face cradling each other. This position leaves their hands free so that they can caress, hug, kiss and stimulate each other. It is restful. It is also the position that is used fairly extensively in Africa. It can allow the partners to cuddle and embrace each other which in itself can extend the enjoyment and intimacy of lovemaking. This position makes it comfortable to fall asleep in each other's arms.

Reverse Side by Side

This is the same position as the face to face except that the man enters from the rear. Many of the same benefits are true and it is also a very gentle form of intercourse. A tightening of the women's thighs can greatly increase stimulation in this position.

Straight Up

This position requires strength, flexibility, and strong back muscles. This position is not designed for long passionate lovemaking. In this position, the woman usually wraps her legs around the man's waist and her arms around his neck. As an assistance, they can lean against an object or a wall in order to steady themselves while they create a rhythm. Or, they can switch things around and allow the man to lean up against the wall. The woman can hold or wrap her arms tightly around his neck and she can create the rhythm by bending her knees and pushing with her feet against the wall. Obviously, this technique should not be tried by the timid or people who are out of condition. **It could be detrimental to your health.**

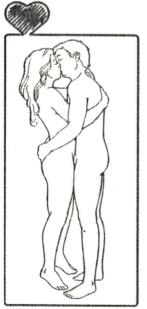

Lap Position

This position has an advantage in that it is not very strenuous on the man or the woman. The woman sits on the man's lap while he is seated. This position probably found a lot of favor with the advent of the drive in movie and the back seat of the car. However, this position has many advantages in that it lends itself easily to brief encounters and has a great number of variations. This position gives good eye contact and allows each partner to view the other's body. It also allows the man to play with the breasts. It also enables people to do a variety of things such as hugging, kissing, caressing, eating or drinking while participating in the sexual encounter.

Every Which Way Variations

People have fantasized about different positions of lovemaking. Books, songs and poems have been written about them. There are numerous positions that can be experimented with. People in the Orient have intercourse while squatting. There are variations of the missionary position where a woman wraps her legs around the man's neck. All of these things can bring additional pleasure and excitement to your relationship. At the same time, certain positions may have physically beneficial advantages. Some positions, because of the nerve endings, cause people to have their bladder stimulated, causing them to urinate either during intercourse or immediately afterwards. Sometimes by changing positions this problem can be alleviated. Experimenting with different positions may have added rewards for those who have been injured, older people or people with arthritis because it can enable them to have the full pleasure and satisfaction of a lasting relationship.

Changing positions will not only enable a person to add variety and spice to their lovemaking, in many cases it will enable them to have satisfying sex until the end of their lives. Thus the pleasure and enjoyment can last and last.

The positions we have described are the standard sex positions from which many others can be derived. There are a great deal of other positions, but basically they are a variation of each of the major positions. The benefit of the positions is an individual preference determined by the comfort and stimulation that it affords to both the man and the woman. You may wish during sexual encounters to experiment with two or three positions during the encounter. A woman can develop muscle tone in her vagina and uterus, which will add an additional sensation to both the man and woman.

Reverse coital alignment. Women can tighten thighs for extra stimulation— use more rocking and pressure to create stimulation and excitement.

In some porn movies or in sex shows people will be fascinated by the fact that a woman is able to control the muscles in her vagina so that she can puff on a pipe or cigar while it inserted in her vagina. This is done through the contractions and expanding of the muscles around the vagina. This is not to say that this is a talent that anyone should try to develop, but it illustrates that women can, if they wish, develop additional muscle tone surrounding the vagina. With practice and training she can bring these muscles under conscientious control and can expertly stoke, squeeze and even pump the penis while it is in the vagina.

The reason a woman can accomplish this is because the walls of the vagina are supported by powerful muscle tissue. While their main function is to hold the vagina and the related structures in place, these muscles can be developed to put an interesting and sensuous aspect on sexual intercourse.

One of the main muscles involved is the vagina sphincter muscle, which is the muscle that surrounds the vaginal opening. This controls the contraction of the vagina. The second pair of muscles are the urethra sphincter muscles. These muscles enable the woman to shut off the flow of urine at the end of urination. They are just inside the vagina outlet.

An easy exercise that a woman can do to gain greater control and muscle tone in this area is by holding back her urine flow then letting it go. The drawing in and releasing of the pelvic muscles exercises the correct structures and gives additional control and tone. If a woman does this on a daily basis, maybe fifteen or twenty times, she will soon see the results. This benefits the woman by increasing her bladder control and muscle tone.

A woman will realize if she needs this additional control by experimentation. She can insert several fingers into her vagina and then, as if she was trying to stop the flow of urine, tighten around those fingers. Pay attention to the amount of pressure. Is it is non-existent, light or does it feel like a large rubber band tightening around your hand? In this way you can gain a general idea of your muscle tone. Having a tight PC muscle not only will enhance pleasure, but is also healthy and beneficial to the woman. Once you've developed additional strength you may want to change the length of contractions. This is a simple exercise that you can do almost anywhere, while you are in the office, driving or sitting at the table eating or in the evening while you are laying in bed.

I will mention that if you are sincerely interested about additional information that you should consult with your doctor. There are products available on the market for women to use in developing additional PC muscle tone. There are things like the Kegelcisor and Femtone along with numerous other items that are readily available at specialty stores.

Once you have developed additional strength in the PC muscles you may then want to try some of the different positions and see what feels best for you. The ultimate result of all this is that you want find the techniques and positions that make you feel most comfortable and create the most sensitivity and excitement during sexual intercourse, so that you will be able to reach the stimulation of the sexual climax and orgasm that you desire to make your sexual encounter fulfilling and pleasing.

Benefits of Variety

Studies have revealed that people who continually renew the romance and variety in their relationship will have more rewarding experiences and pleasures. Both depression and happiness seems to perpetuate themselves. Therefore, when people become flat and burned out on their relationship and their sexual involvement, their anticipation of the experience becomes a detriment and a source of anxiety. Then the physical act lives up to their reduced expectations. The reverse is also true. People who have regular sexual activity, enjoy it, and who are responsive to each other have a tendency to increase their activity and sensitivity and enjoy things more and more together.

Cardinal Rule

No matter how exciting and pleasurable a sex act is, it can become monotonous after a long while.

There are many case studies where people well into their late years have had continued romance and sexual activity in their relationship because it is something they have fostered and nurtured along the way. I am not referring to only the frequency, but also to the quality of the relationship. One of the major facts that was revealed in the interviews is that people who have poor sex will have a tendency to have diminished enjoyment and a reduced sex drive. This will create sources of anxiety and apprehension in the relationship and in some cases is a primary cause of separation, breakup and divorce. The mental anguish that some people put themselves through because of a frustrated love life can be avoided if they take the time and have the patience to understand and develop into their relationship the elements and components that we have discussed in this book.

Cardinal Rule

> **Sexuality and romance continues to the end of life.**

Developing the components we have discussed into your relationship has many advantages. It will help not only strengthen and bring more rewarding responses from your spouse in other day to day activities, it will instill a moral discipline in your relationship and it will have bountiful rewards with your children in creating a healthy family unit and environment with love, care, affection, respect, and happiness. These are all things that when they are practiced in a relationship will perpetuate themselves to the others involved in the family unit and in the relationship. It can make both your sex life as well as your total relationship sweeter.

Chapter XVIII

Anal Sex

This is the position that involves penetration of the anal area from the rear. The reason we mention this is that there are some people who find enjoyment and stimulation in this position. However, in a lot of cases it can be both awkward and painful. It is recommended that you use a Nonoxynol #9 spermicide lubricant and a latex condom when performing anal sex.

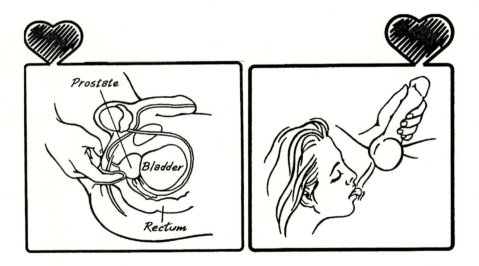

Manual anal sex. Woman can stimulate the male prostate gland to create both an erection and an orgasm. Use a lubricant when penetrating and use more of a caressing motion than thrusting action to stimulate until orgasm.

Sex Toys

Sex toys and sex enhancements go as far back as ancient Egypt. Even primitive tribes have used items made of clay. However, as in all things, when you take a foreign object and put it into the body there is always a danger of it causing damage and pain. There are a great many varieties of items, too many to list. You need your own book today because now there are catalogs with high tech artificial apparatuses that are electronically controlled. But basically, depending on your viewpoint and preference all these items are meant to do one of two things, either enhance sexual pleasures or to create a stimulation to either the man or woman so they may have a sexual climax while they are masturbating. Some of these items are very inventive and in many cases after having reviewed some research information these sex toys may be more of a stimulant to a person's mind and emotions than to their body.

Sometimes people out of curiosity or necessity don't even bother with sex toys, but use items readily at hand like cucumbers and carrots. However, for those of you who do have curiosity, you can pick up a variety of artificial vaginas. Some are wax, some plastic, some inflatable. Some even come with vibrators. The same is true for artificial penises for ladies. Some are made from hard rubber, some are inflatable, and some are filled with hot water which circulates giving the apparatus the illusion of body heat and moistness. They come in a variety of sizes and colors. Some are made of a special gelatin-like material which is very pliable. Some of the penises come with a suction cup. Some models come with a suction cup and vibrator so that the cup can be inserted against the wall or a floor and more representative of an actual penis.

The obvious benefit of these sex toys to both men and women is that it allows them to release sexual tension and anxiety without having to actually engage in sex. Whenever using any of the sex toys that are available on today's market always use good hygiene. Properly clean the items so that there is no chance of them creating an infection. At the same time, make sure that these items aren't physically harmful. The manufacturers of these items many times have no obligations at all and there are documented reports of people having to go to the hospital because of lacerations or painful reactions to sex toys.

Sex toys can be very arousing for couples to use. The idea of edible panties or items that enhance the sexuality of an encounter may cause additional stimulation. Certain lubricants create a variety of sensations and come in a rainbow of flavors such as strawberry, cherry, Irish Crème, passion fruit or cinnamon. There are many massage oils that are scented and have ingredients that will create a warm, tingling feeling when they are massaged into the skin. Sometimes even blowing your warm breath increases heat and sensitivity, causing both externally and internally a new sensation. When these type of items are massaged or rubbed around the nipples, inner thighs, head of the penis or the testicles they can increase both the sensitivity and enjoyment of the experience. If you use an item with mint or peppermint in it, it can add a feeling of tingling warmth while it is being stroked or rubbed on the desired area. As with anything, always be careful with the amounts so that you do not become excessive and cause an irritation or a reaction.

The one concern I would like to bring forth regarding sexual toys is that in some cases they become a crutch for people and replace the pure freedom and joy of a regular sexual encounter to the point where a person is no longer comfortable without the use of certain toys. This is especially true if you get into the more extreme sex toys involving bondage, domination and sado-masochism. These terms are used to cover in a general way sexual activities involving ropes, handcuffs, straps, whips or paddles. It also includes activities where people do unusual or grotesque things with the penis, testicles, vagina or clitoris. A variety of items can be obtained through mail order catalog houses that teach people techniques. Many times these activities are painful and ultimately harmful, both physically and psychologically.

All too often people insert items into their partner's or into their own vagina or rectum that have no business being there. Then there is always the sadist, the person who gets involved with another person to inflict pain, in some perverse way receiving sexual gratification from it. This is the primary reason why I do not go into depth analyzing sex toys. It's simply too easy to misuse many of these items and inflict pain or perhaps even permanent damage on one's partner or even on one's self.

Many become involved with deviant sexual practices and the use of certain sex toys because of gender identity problems. These same characteristics have many times generated tremendous anxiety which builds into a hatred that eventually leads to an emotional explosion. In extreme cases people have maimed and killed other people. You've also seen the pictures in the daily newspapers of people who have kept young children in slavery and bondage. There is always at least some question as to what roles gender identity and sexual frustration have played in such behavior.

For those of you who are interested, there are numerous companies located in the yellow pages that will send you free catalogs/information regarding a variety of sex toys.

The final word is to use some safety factors when choosing. Be careful of the following items:
- The Size—Make sure that it is really appropriate and will not become dangerous.
- The Material—Whether it's plastic, silicone, rubber or metal, it should be something that can be kept clean and not too porous.
- The Shape—Make sure the toy has a practical form so that it does not cause any type of irritation that can lead to additional problems.

Electrical devices always need to be carefully analyzed. Battery powered items are generally safe, but ones needing electrical outlets could become extremely dangerous. You do not want to become a statistic. There are dozens of tales of hapless pleasure seekers who ended up in the E.R. because of an ill fated encounter with a sex toy. When it comes to sex toys, you should never, ever share. Anything that comes in contact with your body and its fluids can come in contact with another person's body and fluids and can transmit sexually transmitted diseases. Therefore, always take proper care of your own sex toys and never share.

Sex toys may not be for everyone, but they can be a lot of fun and add yet another new dimension to sex with your partner.

Chapter XIX

The Real Mission

The real mission of this book is to guide you along that sexual journey so that mistakes, false myths and lack of knowledge will not ruin your relationship and you will be able to obtain the pleasure, satisfaction, enjoyment and excitement that a good sexual relationship should produce.

Reality

There are millions of men and women in our country who are afraid or nervous to talk to their loved ones about their sexual activities, preferences and relationships. This is the major barrier that you must overcome in order to incorporate and instill into your life the elements and components we have discussed in this book. The rewards are mind boggling once you are successful. You can obtain what you may never have obtained except in your fantasies: a truly exciting, pleasurable and rewarding sexual relationship and happiness in your life that will carry on forever and ever.

Most of us want someone who loves us, is faithful and can share a wonderful, fulfilling and pleasurable relationship with us.

There is a great deal more to a sexual relationship than the mere fact of a man and woman having sex. That is what this book is really about. Everyone in their life sooner or later will be faced with developing a good relationship that will result in both their partner's and their own sexual satisfaction. In that way, the relationship will have mutual benefits for both partners.

The successful relationship will have untold benefits. Each partner will receive and gain from the relationship a better self image, a feeling of trust and security, an understanding of what sexuality feels like, and most of all a love that will produce a long term bonding that will give a lifetime of rewards.

If you read this book carefully, you will know most of the important things that are necessary in developing a good and pleasurable sexual relationship. However, you run the risk of having an unexpected or unwanted pregnancy, contracting a fatal sexual transmitted disease, or experiencing untold emotional misery and agony if you rush into a relationship.

We have tried to cover the rules that need to be followed if your sexual relationship is to develop into a pleasant and satisfactory one. You cannot mistreat, abuse, be selfish and uncaring, or produce an unwanted child without eventually experiencing the grief, anguish and misery yourself. So believe that it can happen to you. Think about the main rules and guidelines that we have put in this book in order to help you through that emotional journey in life. Always remember that there is plenty of time to develop a relationship. It is important to be sensitive and caring to the other person's feelings as well as your own. Remember always that developing a sexual relationship involves more than yourself. It involves the feelings, emotions, and life of your partner, the members of your family unit, and perhaps that of a child that will be produced as a result of this relationship. Learn to value both your body, your self esteem and your relationship.

Sensible people will realize they need to control their emotions and sexual behavior and learn to be attentive and responsive to the person they are involved with. We have discussed real problems with real solutions in this book in order to assist you in developing what we are all seeking: a good relationship and terrific sex.

A good sexual relationship is one of the most powerful and deepest relationships that we experience in life. Cherish it and never overlook its importance.

In the beginning of this book, I said life is an emotional journey. I have prepared a road map for you regarding your sexual relationship on that journey. **Pay attention to the guidelines and be sensitive and responsible. This road map can help you avoid the dead ends, detours and worst of all, getting lost on that emotional journey.**

Final Cardinal Rule

> A life time is not too long for love, sex and a relationship!

We would appreciate hearing your comments write to:

RESCUE 911 SERIES Foundation
P.O. Box 511
Troy, Michigan 48099
Free informational brochure: 877-473-9435
Phone Line—877-4 SEX HELP

About the Author

RONALD A. HAGEN is a highly motivated, investigative researcher with over 12 years of experience compiling information regarding sex, love and relationships.

Mr. Hagen was trained as an analyst and researcher while serving as an agent with the Central Intelligence Division. He has adapted this skill to the field of love and relationships, and has spent thousands of hours reviewing facts and theories about relationships. He has exhaustively examined hundreds of exit interviews of couples, has been involved with numerous support groups, and has corresponded with both the federal and state health departments on STDs and relationships. As a result of these experiences, Hagen has been exposed to virtually every theory regarding relationships.

Additionally Mr. Hagen has worked with several school organizations in developing programs for teens. He is co-chairman of the STDs foundation and has worked with the Michigan State Health Department to co-produce television programs regarding teen dating and safe sex. He has written brochures and pamphlets regarding safe sex and abstinence and was featured on cable TV in a half-hour program dealing with the communication and components for developing a successful relationship. He has appeared on the radio for the program Bright Side of Aging and in discussions regarding seniors and their evolving relationships.

Mr. Hagen has conducted seminars and lectures for numerous community organizations. He is the author of *What You Always Wanted to Know About Safe Sex and STDs, The New Teen Dating Game,* and *Love, Sex and Relationships Where Would We Be Without THEM.* He currently teaches courses at Macomb Community College regarding relationships and teen dating.

0-595-20996-3

Printed in the United States
3489